Twayne's United States Authors Series

Sylvia E. Bowman, *Editor*

INDIANA UNIVERSITY

Vladimir Nabokov

TUSAS 266

Vladimir Nabokov

VLADIMIR NABOKOV

By L. L. LEE
Western Washington State College

TWAYNE PUBLISHERS
A Division of G. K. Hall & Co.
Boston, Massachusetts, U. S. A.

1976

Copyright © 1976 by G. K. Hall & Co.
All Rights Reserved
First Printing

Library of Congress Cataloging in Publication Data

Lee, Lawrence L
  Vladimir Nabokov.
  168p. FRONT, 21cm

  (Twayne's United States authors series ; 266)
  Bibliography: p. 161 - 65.
  Includes index.
  1. Nabokov, Vladimir Vladimirovich, 1899-   —Criticism and interpretation.
  PG3476.N3Z7   813'.5'4   76-128
  ISBN 0-8057-7166-2

71737

Contents

About the Author

L. L. Lee received his B.A. (Phi Beta Kappa), M.A., and Ph.D. from the University of Utah, where he concentrated on modern languages and literature. He is at present Professor of English at Western Washington State College in Bellingham, Washington, and teaches a variety of courses in modern British and American literature, among which is a regular class on Vladimir Nabokov.

Mr. Lee is editor of the critical journal, *Concerning Poetry*. He has published a monograph, *Walter Van Tilburg Clark*, on the work of that American writer. His critical essays (three on Nabokov and others on such artists as C. P. Cavafy, James Joyce, Thomas Berger, and E. M. Forster), stories, translations (from French and modern Greek), and poems have appeared in over two dozen American journals, including *Contemporary Literature*, *Western Humanities Review*, *Poetry* (Chicago), *College English*, and *Studies in Short Fiction*.

Preface

The works of Vladimir Nabokov form a single entity that contain certain basic motifs and subjects which are inextricably intertwined with the man's own experience and with his life as a creative artist. As a result, his works continually look forward and backward; and they continually connect, not only within themselves and with each other, but with his vital and artistic concerns. The central vital and artistic theme of this study of his work is that the experience of the artist is the experience of being truly human; for the artist is the exemplar not only of man as creator, in a sense separate from the world of "fact," but also of man in actuality, that is, man in time. We should not, however, reduce all of Nabokov's concerns to that simple statement; for his are varied and complex interests that change in time — for example, his change of artistic language, from Russian to English, in itself gives another world view.

Nabokov makes connections by a repetition of specifics. For this reason, the first part of this study is a kind of biography — the biography Nabokov himself has given which expresses his concerns most clearly in his memoir, *Speak, Memory*. *Speak, Memory* is not a confession; it is, rather, a work of art which presents the development of the artist. Therefore, the biography that I sketch in Chapter 1 demonstrates this development of, as well as the themes of, the artist. Because Nabokov says that "Imagination is a form of memory,"[1] the succeeding chapters are a more or less chronological examination of the fiction, the short stories, and the novels, each of which grows out of and refers back to the others. These works give artistic shape to the vision expressed in Nabokov's life. The author's poems, plays, critical works, and certain minor novels, such as *The Eye* and *Transparent Things*, are considered only as they relate to his more important works. The novel *Look at the Harlequins!* (1974) is almost an allegory of Nabokov's life as an artist; but, since it too is minor, I use it only as an illustration of the themes of *Ada*. Athough most of the Russian novels, except *The Gift*, are not equal to Nabokov's two major English novels, *Lolita* and *Pale Fire*, I treat them at some length because they develop his themes. My summary chapter repeats those themes and argues for Nabokov's place in literary history.

We could begin a presentation of the unifying themes of Nabokov's work by referring to the critical reception of his novels, for this reception has been and is intimately related to what he is and believes. Although, for instance, most English-speaking critics agree that he is an important writer, there is considerably less agreement upon how important Nabokov really is. There is probably less agreement upon whether he is a Russian, an American, or a "cosmopolitan" writer. But the conflict over his importance and his tradition is, in essence, an argument over art or, more precisely, how art is related to life. This "relationship" is not only a continuing concern but a continuing subject in every work by Nabokov. For critics and readers who believe that literature must have an explicit social or religious or moral purpose in a particular moment and culture, Nabokov can seem cold and inhuman and therefore unimportant. However, Nabokov is a great writer for those critics and readers such as myself who believe that literature must not be reduced to such narrow purposes, for it exists in itself at the same moment that it examines humanity and the cosmos. For he is concerned above all with the *making of* and the *made* work of art as it is related to other works of art, especially in its linguistic and cultural tradition. That is, he is concerned with the work of art as experience in itself for the reader or spectator as well as with what it "says" about man in the universe.

Nabokov himself, through his own statements in interviews and in his various introductions to his English works, has contributed mightily to the argument over his place in literature. He has seemingly refused to compromise; literature is not "utilitarian" — although he has said, in an interview in 1971, that "I believe that one day a reappraiser will come and declare that, far from having been a frivolous firebird, I was a rigid moralist kicking sin, cuffing stupidity, ridiculing the vulgar and cruel — and assigning sovereign power to tenderness, talent, and pride . . . . [and there is not] really so much doom and 'frustration' in my fiction [as some have thought]. . . ."[2] And, indeed, Nabokov is, if not a rigid moralist, certainly a moralist; but his "morality" is both human and artistic.

For Nabokov's work is human and useful, not despite its art but because of it. One of my aims is, therefore, to demonstrate by showing how the themes become form, and how form becomes theme, that his work *embodies* human meaning. As Vladislav Khodasevich has observed, when speaking of Nabokov's writing. "Art cannot be reduced to form, but without form it has no existence and, consequently, no meaning. Therefore the analysis of a work of art is unthinkable without an analysis of form."[3]

As I have suggested, the esthetic ideas of Nabokov would seem to be a variant on an "art-for-art's-sake" esthetic. When he says "Although I do not care for the slogan 'art for art's sake' . . . there can be no question that what makes a work of fiction safe from larvae and rust is not its social importance but its art, only its art,"[4] he seems to separate art from history — from man's life in time and community — and to make art a pure object without direct human significance. This quotation reveals, however, something of Nabokov's larger concerns. The allusion to Matthew 6:19 about this "earth, where moth and rust doth corrupt," makes the quotation a part of cultural history, since it thereby enters into literary and religious history; but it also suggests that Nabokov accepts a kind of Platonic "idea" of art — even though we must beware of carrying this relationship too far, since Plato, who is a generalizer and who would keep artists in their place, is one of those people Nabokov cannot abide. Nonetheless, a realm of permanent artistic values exists for Nabokov; and all fiction must somehow be part of that realm if it is to be more than mere motion.

Nabokov's values are, nevertheless, basically anthropocentric, not transcendental. If he asserts that "great literature skirts the irrational,"[5] he does not mean that its first subject or concern is with the supernatural, the other worldly, the mystical; but neither does he mean that its concern is with some kind of depth psychology, some methodical probing of the "psychology" of man, for the irrational is not to be explained by Freudian, or even Jungian, determinisms. Rather, art gives us insights into our "place" in the world — insights that, indeed, reason cannot give us. But art works in its own way, by its own order. Therefore, Nabokov's "stress is not on the mystery but on the pattern";[6] for it is through the pattern of art that the artist discovers the mystery. To Nabokov, literature arrives at the mystery by indirection, by seeking out the patterns, by making patterns, but always human patterns. Alternatively, we can say that art orders us — and orders the world for us.

Literature, then, is from life, but it is also from other literature, since the great artists — Alexander Pushkin, William Shakespeare, and.Nikolai Gogol, to name three of the writers Nabokov admires most — were men with this strange insight and control over the mystery. They gave us insights that we can not only experience but use — in art, in patterns. For this reason, we must point out how and why Nabokov uses other artists despite the fact that the individual artist is always separate, separate and himself. To Nabokov, "The quiddity of individual artistic achievement . . . alone matters and alone survives. . . ."[7] Still, by bringing together the various patterns of life, of art, and of his allusions to other artists, I shall show how Nabokov's works connect with one another and with his life; and I shall do so not in order to demonstrate that he is being "autobiographical" in his works but that he is joining his worlds with ours.

But perhaps the best statements of Nabokov's ideas about the writer, about the writer's subjects, about the reader, and about how art orders can be found in the following quotations:

A creative writer . . . must possess the inborn capacity not only of recombining but of re-creating the given world. In order to do this adequately . . . the artist should know the given world. Imagination without knowledge leads no farther than the backyard of primitive art. . . . Art is never simple.[8]

In art as in science there is no delight without the detail . . . . unless these are thoroughly understood and remembered, all "general ideas" (so easily acquired, so profitably resold) must necessarily remain but worn passports allowing their bearers short cuts from one area of ignorance to another.[9]

Give me the creative reader. . . .[10]

Since form cannot, of course, be separated from language, we must agree that we cannot really understand the work of Nabokov without some idea of what he wrote in Russian. In the analyses of the English version of his Russian works, I make references to the Russian originals, as well as to the language itself, in order to show how Nabokov's Russian background, both in language and in culture, has made him the writer he is in English as well as in Russian.

Nabokov is not a theoretician; there is no book in which he has developed his esthetics at length. But his ideas on art are ubiquitous in his writings. Most of the statements about his esthetics in this study are derived from his statements in such works as his *Gogol*, which contains the most complete exposition of his views about art; from *Speak, Memory*; from his introductions to his novels; from his

Preface

notes to his "literal" translation of Pushkin's *Eugene Onegin*; and from his comments in various interviews. We should add that the reason for the many direct quotes is that his style is inimitable and often cannot be easily paraphrased without distortion.

But I have occasionally quoted or used "ideas" of one of his characters as though they were his. There is a danger to this process, since an author is not his creature, and since Nabokov himself has spoken witheringly of an "anonymous clown, writing on *Pale Fire*. . . , who mistook all the declarations of my invented commentator in the book for my own." But in all such cases I present some supporting evidence, some suggestion by Nabokov that he agrees with his character — as in this instance: "It is also true that some of my more responsible characters are given some of my own ideas. There is John Shade in *Pale Fire*, the poet. He does borrow some of my own opinions"[11] — or some assertion of Nabokov elsewhere — that reinforces what the character has said. Although we must consider Nabokov's discouragement of "idea" hunting in his works, a critic cannot ignore the work itself; and, if the work touches upon, explores, or realizes "ideas," those "ideas" must be discussed despite the author's admonition. On the other hand, the emphasis in this study is upon the works, not on an abstractable "message"; for Nabokov's works in their wholeness are what matters.

Finally, I should like to thank those who have helped me write this book, above all my wife, Sylvia; second, Vladimir Milicic, who read and explained the Russian works to me; and, lastly, those many critics and scholars, upon whose work I have freely depended.

L. L. LEE

Western Washington State College

Acknowledgments

I wish to thank those named for permission to quote from the following books to which they hold copyright.

Vladimir Nabokov for quotations from *Nikolai Gogol* and *Speak Memory*; McGraw-Hill Book Company for quotations from *Ada, King, Queen, Knave, Mary,* and *Poems and Problems*; New Directions Publishing Company for quotations from *Laughter in the Dark* and *The Real Life of Sebastian Knight*.

I would also like to thank the following for permission to quote from my own articles to which they hold the copyright: The Regents of the University of Wisconsin and the editors of *Studies in Short Fiction* and *The Western Humanities Review*.

Chronology

1899   Vladimir Nabokov born (April 10, Julian calendar; April 22, Gregorian calendar) in St. Petersburg, Russia; eldest child of Vladimir Dmitrievich and Elena Ivanovna (Rukavishnikov) Nabokov.

1913 - Attends Tenishev School, St. Petersburg.
1916

1916   *Poems*, privately printed.

1919   Nabokov family flees Russia; Nabokov, in England, enters Cambridge.

1922   Nabokov's father assassinated by right-wing Russians in Berlin.

1923   Nabokov graduated from Cambridge with honors; goes to Berlin.

1925   Married Vera Evseevna Slonim.

1926   First novel, *Mashenka*, published under penname of V. Sirin.

1928   *Korol', Dama, Valet* (King, Queen, Knave).

1929   *Zashchita Luzhina* (The Defense) published serially; appears as book in 1930.

1930   *Vozvrashchenie Chorba* (The Return of Chorb). Stories and poems.

1932   *Podvig* (Glory); *Kamera Obskura* (Laughter in the Dark).

1934   Nabokovs' only child, Dmitri, born.

1936   *Otchayanie* (Despair).

1937 - *Dar* (The Gift) appeared serially in *Sovremennye Zapiski*
1938   (Contemporary Notes) without the fourth chapter. Nabokovs move to Paris.

1938   *Priglashenie na Kazn'* (Invitation to a Beheading).

1940   Nabokovs sail on liner *Champlain* for United States just escaping invading Germans.

1941   *The Real Life of Sebastian Knight*, Nabokov's first English novel.

1942   Nabokov teaches at Wellesley College; serves as a research fellow in the Museum of Comparative Zoology at Harvard.

1944   *Nikolai Gogol*, critical memoir.

1945   Nabokov becomes an American citizen.

1947   *Bend Sinister*.

1948   Teaches Russian and European literature at Cornell University.

1951   *Conclusive Evidence* (first version of *Speak, Memory*), memoir.

1954   *Drugie berega* (Other Shores), translation into Russian and expansion of *Conclusive Evidence*.

1955   *Lolita* published in Paris.

1957   *Pnin*.

1958   *Lolita* published in the United States; *Nabokov's Dozen*, short stories, published.

1960   Nabokovs move to Montreux, Switzerland; Nabokov retains his American citizenship.

1962   *Pale Fire*.

1964   Translation of Pushkin's *Eugene Onegin*.

1966   *Speak, Memory: An Autobiography Revisited*, an expansion of *Conclusive Evidence* and *Drugie berega*. *Nabokov's Quartet*, short stories.

1969   *Ada*.

1972   *Transparent Things*.

1973   *A Russian Beauty*, short stories.

1973   *Strong Opinions*, essays and interviews.

1974   *Look at the Harlequins!*

1974   *Lolita: A Screenplay*.

1975   *Tyrants Destroyed and Other Stories*, short stories.

CHAPTER 1

An Artist's Life

V LADIMIR Vladimirovich Nabokov, Russian and American
novelist, poet, scholar, translator, esthetician, lepidopterist,
chess player, and tennis coach, was born the eldest child of five to
Vladimir Dmitrievich and Elena Ivanovna (Rukavishnikov) Nabokov
in St. Petersburg, Russia, on April 10, 22, and 23, 1899. These dates
are not a joke, although Nabokov himself is a great comedian; they
are real, complex and simple, paradoxical and plain, and a key as
well as a puzzle — a key to place, to family, and to what Nabokov
was to become. Time, place, family, and identities are important to
him in a way they are not to most writers; for they are his subject
matter and his form. They — that is, "time, space, and matter (that
Lesser Trinity),"[1] — are what would be Nabokov's final concern if
he were not more interested in "reality," in life, in his and other
men's places in that lesser trinity. The dates, therefore, are a way
into the artist's concerns, into his writings. On the one level, of
course, these dates are simple. By the Julian calendar, still being
used in imperial Russia in 1899, the day was April 10; by the
Gregorian calendar used in Western Europe, it was April 22; but by
the Gregorian calendar in the twentieth century — when it gains
another day on the Julian — it would be April 23; and this April 23 is
used on Nabokov's passport.

But there is, in Nabokov's works, and despite his own often-
repeated protestations, no easy and clear distinction between the artist's life and the artist's work; and the emphasis is upon the word *artist*, not upon the man himself. His life and his work are from the
beginning paradoxical and ambiguous; for the work is a way of controlling the life: "Average reality begins to rot and stink as soon as
the act of individual creation ceases to animate a subjectively
perceived texture."[2] Although, on the one hand, it is true that "it is

pretty useless to deduce the life history and human form of a poet from his work; and the greater the artist the more likely it is for us to arrive at erroneous conclusions,"[3] it is more than useful, on the other hand, to deduce the form of the works from the life of the artist, if that artist is Nabokov. "Imagination is a form of memory," as he says;[4] and "I doubt whether you can even give your telephone number without giving something of yourself."[5]

Louis D. Rubin argues that *Lolita* is not an autobiographical work "because no authorial personality is involved."[6] In other words, the author is not the narrator, Humbert Humbert; but there is always an authorial personality in Nabokov's works in that Nabokov, as the creator, as the god perhaps of his fictional world, is directly communicating to the reader. Moreover, he is involving the reader, not with the sufferings of the author's body and soul, but with the play of his mind, the actual act of creation. As a result, the reader must make the same connections as the author; he must reach from work to work, from life to work; he must, in short, become, as Nabokov has also said his ideal readers should be, "little Nabokovs."[7]

I Speak, Memory

Nabokov's memoir, *Speak, Memory*,[8] provides factual knowledge of and insight into the complex figure that Nabokov is, or, rather, into the artist, the persona that is Nabokov. What the memoir presents is the portrait, not of the man, but of the artist as man. *Speak, Memory* is not a simple chronological detailing of the facts of the author's life — instead, it is a made object, a work of art in itself. As a kind of fiction, it is dependent upon certain objective facts and events; but these facts and events yield significance only by making "the lamp of art . . . shine through life's foolscap" (25). In short, Nabokov is trying to understand his life as well as to preserve it.

The memoir is primarily concerned with the thirty-seven years from August, 1903, to May, 1940; and it is, therefore, limited in time and subject matter. But these years are continually present in Nabokov's work, even in those "American" works such as *Lolita*; and the book's organization, its intricate interweaving of pasts with the present, is the pattern of the novels. For example, a particular chapter may be built upon a single subject: the family's daily life; his tutors; Mademoiselle, his unforgettable French governess; his butterfly pursuits; his first intense love affair with a girl he calls Tamara, whose avatars will appear again and again; the university years at Cambridge; his writing. But he does not mention either his meeting the girl who would become his wife or the ceremony of their marriage — although he repeatedly speaks of her, addresses her and their son. What he does do is to explore those moments of his life that are most meaningful to his art as well as to himself; the memoir is not a confession, but rather the vision which informs his whole creative life.

This vision is summed up in his birthdates: they are time made concrete, but they are also demonstrations of the complexity of the simple and illustrations of a pattern that pulls the complexity together. We must add that this accident of misdating as a result of "being shifted by revolution and expatriation" (13) is more than an accident; it is the first of Nabokov's "fatidic" dates, those moments of time that tie the seemingly disparate together, for April 23 is also "the birth date of Shakespeare, my nephew Vladimir Sikorski, Shirley Temple and Hazel Brown (who, moreover, shares my passport)" (13 - 14). That Harold, Charlotte, and Lolita Haze of *Lolita* and that Hazel Shade of *Pale Fire* may share their names with the color of Nabokov's eyes or that, in *Lolita*, one of Clare Quilty's pseudonyms or "motelonyms" is Will Brown of Dolores, Colorado, the brown that was the color of the younger Nabokov's hair, are perhaps of only passing interest; but that fatidic dates relate Nabokov to Shakespeare (and to Pushkin, who believed in them) is of great importance. For these two greatest of poets, in Nabokov's eyes, are an intimate element of his works. Or, in short, if Nabokov's life is an inextricable part of his art, so is the whole body of Art, especially the art of literature.

As Nabokov's own John Shade, the father of Hazel Shade, puts it:

> I feel I understand
> Existence, or at least a minute part
> Of my existence, only through my art,
> In terms of combinational delight.[9]

The combinations are patterns perceived and/or created by the human mind. And they exist everywhere, in fiction and in the "real" world. What Nabokov himself says of Pushkin's life and work applies to his own: "As so often happens with well-studied lives, an artistically satisfying pattern appears. . . ."[10]

But birthdates are not just dates of physical birth; there are also births of consciousness, of humanity. And Nabokov's later birthdate of consciousness was his first awareness of time, that time which is, as I have suggested, a major concern of his art: time, he says, is a spherical prison without exits; timelessness is freedom. When, on a certain day in his fourth year, he recognized that his parents and he were in time, he had a tremendously invigorating shock; for, he asserts, mankind's "reflexive consciousness" was born with his "sense of time" (20 - 21).

However, if Nabokov's actual birthdate is important, his birthplace is equally so, if in a different sense. Nabokov's personal fortune and misfortune, but surely his artistic fortune, was to have been born to a rich and old family in St. Petersburg. A Russian city with a German name, more than half-foreign and artificially created,[11] St. Petersburg was still Russia's capital; and its eye was on the West. St. Petersburg, as a city, has kept for Nabokov the quality of magic that it had when he was a child; and its image, especially its winter image, appears throughout his fiction as nostalgic symbol of time passing and yet of time stopped.

This birthplace and this birthright gave Nabokov a Russian childhood and his "natural idiom, my untrammeled, rich, and infinitely docile Russian tongue."[12] But this childhood was also English, for he learned to read English before he did Russian. Since he also learned French, he commands two other languages, both of which he speaks with an accent but which he writes fluently. This birthplace also gave him a sudden view of revolution and then of exile. The Russian Revolution or, rather, the "Soviet dictatorship," deprived him, he says, of his childhood, which he regrets intensely, and of his money, which he claims not to regret.

Nabokov's repeated use of his past is not, we must emphasize, a sentimental desire to return to it; but nostalgia, a most human emotion, enters into his work. Nevertheless, if past time is recaptured, it is for something else than mere recapture. In fact, since "imagination is a form of memory," Nabokov asserts,

Down, Plato, down, good dog. An image depends on the power of association, and association is supplied and prompted by memory. When we speak of a vivid individual recollection we are paying a compliment not to our capacity of retention but to Mnemosyne's mysterious foresight in having stored up this or that element which creative imagination may use when combining it with later recollections and inventions. In this sense, both memory and imagination are a negation of time.[13]

Nabokov's recognition of himself and his parents helped to place him in the actual world. To recognize the actual world is to locate ourselves; and, paradoxically, by knowing the outside, we know the inside. And so Nabokov's family interests him not merely for the sake of his ego. It is an old family, a very "Russian" one — that is, it is not pure Slavic. The founder probably was a "Russianized Tatar prince in Muscovy," Nabok Murza, who lived circa 1380 (52) — and a certain Nabok has a moment of life in Nabokov's *Ada*. However, the family does not really enter Russian history until the latter half of the eighteenth century, after which time it produced a great number of military men and statesmen. Too, Nabokov traces one line to the German composer, Carl Heinrich Graun, of whom he is proud since Graun is an artist, although Nabokov claims to have no ear for music (his son Dmitri, though, entered upon a career in opera). But what we should see in this family tree is the cosmopolitanism which is an integral part of Nabokov's world view. And, if his mother's family was less cosmopolitan in ancestry, it was not necessarily more "Russian." For it was comprised of "Siberian pioneers, gold prospectors and mining engineers" (66); in other words, they were rather more "progressive," more European or even American, than the usual Russian.

Nabokov's father, Vladimir Dmitrievich Nabokov, to whom he was very close and who introduced him to the world of nature, especially lepidoptery, was hardly the autocratic Russian father of legend. He was a strong, decent man who respected other people; and he gave his son his values. Vladimir Dmitrievich was one of the founders of the Constitutionalist Democratic Party, the so-called Cadets, a liberal bourgeois-landowner party opposed not only to Tsarist absolutism but also to violent revolution; for this group wished to bring about changes in Russia by reform. Nabokov's father's political ideas, and attitudes lie behind Nabokov's, behind his acts and his works; Nabokov himself describes his political beliefs thusly.

. . . since my youth — I was 19 when I left Russia — my political outlook has remained as bleak and changeless as an old gray rock. It is classical to the point of triteness. Freedom of speech, freedom of thought, freedom of art. The social or economic structure of the ideal state is of little concern to me. My desires are modest. Portraits of the head of the government should not exceed a postage stamp in size. No torture and no executions. No music, except coming through earphones, or played in theaters.[14]

Nabokov's family spent most of its summers at its country estate, Vyra, some fifty miles to the south of St. Petersburg. This northwestern Russian landscape, with the Oredezh River running through the Nabokov and Rukavishnikov estates; these flowers; these birches and firs; these mushrooms; and, above all, these butterflies haunt Nabokov's work — and, in a sense, his vision of himself. Alfred Appel, Jr., reports that in 1966 Nabokov, after reading from Alexander B. Klots' *A Field Guide to the Butterflies* the statement that "The recent work of Nabokov has entirely rearranged the classification of" the Lycaeides genus, remarked, "That's real fame. That means more than anything a literary critic could say."[15] Nabokov makes almost the same assertion in his English poem, "A Discovery," in which all of man's cultural and political endeavors only "ape" the "immortality" of the label on a specimen butterfly.[16]

In winter, the Nabokovs usually returned to their town house in St. Petersburg and to that other Russian landscape, the snow-blurred, sun-bright city among its canals. But there were, too, magic trips to the south of France, to Italy, to the Adriatic — to those places where rich Russians went to escape Russia — although Nabokov himself never felt that need. On one of these trips, to Biarritz in 1909, Nabokov met the little girl whom he calls Colette in *Speak, Memory.* This story of young love takes only four pages in the memoir; but Colette's ghosts, like the Russian butterflies, forever accompany him. She becomes, for example, the model for the Annabel of *Lolita*, a brilliant example of how a memory of childhood, mere experience, can be metamorphosed by art into something rich and strange. Nabokov later denied the "affinities" between Colette and Annabel, especially the sexual element, by pointing out that he was only ten when he met Colette and that Humbert Humbert was thirteen and pubescent when he knew Annabel.[17] We must admit that the artistic world is not just a re-presentation of the biographical world; however, the "affinities," the connections between the two worlds, do exist; for all things the artist knows connect.

On these trips the Nabokovs were accompanied by governesses, usually English; later, in Russia, there was the remarkable (in Nabokov's recreation of her) Mademoiselle and then a series of Russian tutors from all parts of the Russian empire. Usually liberal, even radical, but decent young men, they must have suffered from the attitudes of the adolescent, proud Nabokov. For, when Nabokov attended, between 1913 and 1916, the liberal Prince Tenishev School which, in trying to be democratic, insisted upon the students' "conforming to [their] surroundings" (185), the young Nabokov rebelled against this equalism. His own liberalism could neither then, nor later, accept the idea of all being the same, or of their doing and thinking the same; for he objected to having to join "movements or associations of any kinds" (186). As he has remarked, "I . . . have despised ideological coercion instinctively all my life."[18] This attitude, of course, informs his second English novel, *Bend Sinister*.

In his adolescence, he also experienced his first real love affair, one with the girl Tamara. Tamara was from a lower class; no doubt she and Nabokov would never have married, despite his own insistence to her that they would; but the Revolution parted them forever. Like others he knew, Tamara became part of his fictional world; she, for example, is the model for Mashenka (Mary) in his first novel *Mashenka*; and their story is the story, almost, of Lev Ganin and Mashenka.

Nabokov had a happy childhood, one he looks back to with a pervading sense of loss. He was, of course, rich; he was loved; his family was, at least on the surface, stable and happy. However, his story of his brother Sergei, in the revised *Speak, Memory*, suggests that for Sergei life was intensely miserable and that his death was tragic — he died in a Nazi concentration camp of starvation. He too affected Nabokov's fiction; as Page Stegner points out, there are "certain parallels" between Nabokov and Sergei and V. and Sebastian in *The Real Life of Sebastian Knight*.[19] At the end of 1916, Nabokov's maternal uncle "Ruka" died, leaving Nabokov approximately two million dollars and a country estate which were lost in the Revolution. With the Revolution, the Nabokov family fled first to Yalta, a place which plays its part in such books as *The Eye*. In 1919, the Nabokovs escaped Russia in an old Greek ship called the *Nadezhda* (Hope); and there is a fine, cosmopolitan irony about this Greek ship with such a Russian name. After stopping in Constantinople, they went to Greece where they spent two spring months — and where Nabokov pursued butterflies. This journey provides the landscape, if not the events, for his fifth novel, *Podvig (Glory)*. From Greece, the Nabokovs went to Europe. In England, Nabokov entered Cambridge University, supported by scholarships; there he studied French and Russian literature and tried to make himself a Russian writer — he had already published two books of poems in Russia, juvenile poems which he later rejected.

These Cambridge years were, in a sense, confused ones although Nabokov himself was apparently never unsure of himself. He took part in university life, social and physical; but at the same time he was entirely apart. Symbolic, perhaps, of his life in these years was that, although he played soccer, he preferred to be the goalkeeper. Lonely, alone, proud, self-sufficient, he leaned on a goalpost "composing verse in a tongue nobody understood" (268). This sense of proud loneliness he gives to certain of his fictional creatures: to Timofey Pnin, for instance, and then, ironically, to Charles Kinbote, the madman. But, of course, Nabokov's most direct use of Cambridge is in *Podvig* and in the first English novel, *The Real Life of Sebastian Knight*.

More important to his life, though, than Cambridge, was the death of his father on the evening of March 22, 1922. While attending a liberal political meeting in Berlin, the elder Nabokov was shot by two Russian rightwingers who had intended to kill another man. This murder, with all its ambiguities, remains with Nabokov; it became at least an element in the death of John Shade in *Pale Fire* nearly forty years later, for that death is perhaps the result of an error. And we must note here that Nabokov published all his Russian works under the pen name V. Sirin since he felt that his beloved father had previous rights as an author to the name of Vladimir Nabokov.

After graduation from Cambridge, Nabokov moved to Berlin. There, in 1925, he married Vera Evseevna Slonim; and they had one son, Dmitri, in 1934. It has been a most successful marriage; and, once more, despite the dangers of basing everything in an author's works upon his life, it is impossible to avoid the sense that the Zina Mertz of *Dar (The Gift)* is in part modeled upon Mrs. Nabokov. A year after his marriage, Nabokov's first novel, *Mashenka*, was published; and, during the next eleven years, he published all of his Russian novels. But, since his writing brought him very little money, he had to make his living variously, largely by teaching English to German businessmen and tennis to their daughters — which Martin Edelweiss, the protagonist of *Podvig*, also does. Nabokov helped write a Russian grammar for foreigners, and he created the first Russian crossword puzzles for émigré Russian newspapers. These puzzles and the chess problems he worked out are metaphors for his novels. *The Defense*, for instance, is not only about chess but has chess interwoven into its very flesh, its words. And he sold a translation into Russian of *Alice in Wonderland* for the sum of five dollars, "quite a sum during the inflation in Germany" (283). But, of course, *Alice* gave him more than five dollars: the insane and logical voice of Lewis Carroll permeates his works.

Then, in 1937, the Nabokovs left Germany for Paris because Nabokov objected to the "nauseous dictatorship"[20] of Hitler but also because Mrs. Nabokov is Jewish. Racism, in life or in fiction, is abhorrent to Nabokov; indeed, Alfred Appel gives Nabokov's story of his walking out of an American restaurant which discriminated against Jews: it was not an act of physical courage but an act of the spirit. "My son was very proud of me," Nabokov said.[21]

In 1937 - 1938, he published *Dar (The Gift)* in an émigré journal, and this work was his last Russian novel. Although he now began to write seriously in French and in English, the French works are limited; but they do include the first version of Chapter 5 of *Speak, Memory*, the story of his governess, Mademoiselle O. He had decided that his future was as an English writer, and in 1938 he made the first draft of *The Real Life of Sebastian Knight*. But the changeover in languages was a terrible wrench:

My private tragedy, which cannot, and indeed should not, be anybody's concern, is that I had to abandon my natural idiom, my untrammeled, rich, and infinitely docile Russian tongue for a second-rate brand of English, devoid of any of those apparatuses — the baffling mirror, the black velvet backdrop, the implied associations and traditions — which the native illusionist, frac-tails flying, can magically use to transcend the heritage in his own way.[22]

Nabokov's love for the Russian language is more than a concern for "tradition," if we use that word in the narrow sense of simply conserving the past. A language is a world, and a literature is part of that world: to regard literature only as "sense" is, in essence, to hate literature. A translation can never convey the delicacies, the richness, the weight of words. But, we should also add that the structure of Russian probably fits Nabokov's concerns with time better than English does; therefore, his change of language is a loss. As he says, "There are words rendering certain nuances of motion and gesture and emotion in which Russian excels. Thus by changing the head of a verb, for which one may have a dozen different prefixes to choose from, one is able to make Russian express extremely fine shades of duration and intensity."[23]

On May 28, 1940, the Nabokovs sailed on the *Champlain* from St. Nazaire for the United States. Here *Speak, Memory* ends. In America, Nabokov became a teacher, first at Wellesley, "where I taught college girls Russian grammar and literature."[24] There is an echo of his teaching experiences in his best English poem, "An

Evening of Russian Poetry," as well as in *Pnin* and *Pale Fire*. From 1942 until 1948; he also was, as an expert on the *Lepidoptera*, a research fellow at the Museum of Comparative Zoology at Harvard; and during these years he published a number of articles about butterflies.

In 1941, he published *The Real Life of Sebastian Knight* after, as he has had acknowledged, he had several native English speakers look at the manuscript and give him advice.[25] In 1945, he became an American citizen. But these first years in America were relatively sterile so far as creative work was concerned. It was not until 1947 that *Bend Sinister*, the first novel he wrote while in America, appeared; this, his most "political" novel is, in a way, a recording of the dark demons of the European politics of his earlier life. In 1948, he went to Cornell University, where he remained until 1959 when *Lolita* made it possible for him to give up teaching. During all these American years, he traveled the United States on butterfly-hunting trips; *Lolita* was not only partly written on those trips but got its geography from them. He was absorbing America and becoming an American writer.

However, although he has retained his American citizenship, the Nabokovs have lived in Montreux, Switzerland, since 1960; their primary motive for returning to Europe was to be near their son, who was there to study opera. But this move has been a much less significant break in Nabokov's personal and artistic lives than other such moves, for he did not stop being an American writer. Asked in 1966 if the classification of himself as Russian or American mattered, Nabokov replied: "I have always maintained, even as a schoolboy in Russia, that the nationality of a worthwhile writer is of secondary importance. . . . The writer's art is his real passport. His identity should be immediately recognized by a special pattern or unique coloration. . . . Apart from these considerations I think of myself today as an American writer who has once been a Russian one."[26]

II *Language and the Spiral Image*

Still, Nabokov's cosmopolitanism, his being "a person at home in any country,"[27] is more than just a multiplication of experience; it is at the center of his sense of language. However, Nabokov, almost incredibly sensitive to language, of what it can and cannot do, recognizes not only that both his art and he himself are absolutely dependent upon it but also that language is not everything. In one of the imaginary conversations that the hero, Fyodor Godunov-

Cherdyntsev (who is a positive artist-figure and therefore an aspect of his creator) of *The Gift* has with the poet Koncheyev, Koncheyev accuses Fyodor of having "an excessive trust in words."[28] But Nabokov himself admits that people "think not in words"; they think in images.[29] Alfred Appel quite rightly argues that Nabokov is objecting to "the burden the post-Romantics placed on the word, as though it were an endlessly resonant object rather than one component in a referential system of signs." For example Nabokov objected to Joyce's "giving 'too much verbal body to words.'"[30] Despite Nabokov's overwhelming concern with words, then, his epistemology is at bottom object-centered, not word-centered.

But, in the end, words are all we have to define ourselves and with which to communicate. A 1927 Russian poem, "V Rayu," or "In Paradise," speaks of what it would be like to be a "provincial naturalist" in Paradise who comes across a "wild angel . . . , /a semi-pavonian creature" and who suddenly remembers that, since there are neither readers nor journals in Paradise, he can only stare in terrible despair "at those unnamable [anonymous] wings."[31]

One of the most brilliant early insights into Nabokov's works is that of the remarkable émigré poet and critic Vladislav Khodasevich who pointed out in his 1937 article, "On Sirin," that "the life of the artist and the life of a device in the consciousness of the artist — this is Sirin's theme, revealing itself to some degree or other in almost every one of his writings, beginning with *The Defense*."[32] Khodasevich does qualify his assertion by adding that Nabokov never makes use of "actual" artists; instead, he chooses a "mask: a chess-player, a business man, etc." Perhaps what Khodasevich should have said is that Nabokov never makes use of the successful artist, for he sometimes presents the failed artist as hero, for example Hermann Karlovich in *Despair*. Such a failed artist has put too much faith in the act of art, for he has believed that it, language, could manipulate "reality."

But this relation between Nabokov's life and his art is best explained by an examination of the ruling image of his art, and Nabokov himself offers us the figure: In *Speak, Memory*, he says that he sees his life as a "colored spiral in a small ball of glass" and that the spiral is the circle "set free" to give us a visual form for the Hegelian triad — thesis, antithesis, synthesis. All things, he adds, are essentially spiral "in their relation to time." Therefore, "The twenty years I spent in my native Russia (1899 - 1919) take care of the thetic arc. Twenty-one years of voluntary exile in England, Germany and

France (1919 - 1940) supply the obvious antithesis. The period spent in my adopted country (1940 - 1960) forms a synthesis — and a new thesis" (275).

It may be that pure chance (whatever that is) determined that his life would fall so neatly into such patterns; but the artist's mind perceived those patterns. Still, to assert that the figure an author applies to his life also applies to his art is not, of course, sufficient; we must show that it does apply and that it does explain. For the moment, let me say that the spiral does throw light on those mirror-reflections, *doppelgängers*, chess games, spelling reversals, puns, repetitions of situations, sexual ambivalences, and echoes of names that we find in Nabokov's fiction. For the spiral is like the circle, but it is less exact, less rigid; it is time recurring and yet not quite; events that are repeated but only partially; mirror images that are of necessity distorted because they exist at different moments. The spiral is the figure of space and time unified, but a figure that allows multiplicity in its unity. The "V" (Vladimir?) of *Sebastian Knight* says that, to Sebastian, "time and space were . . . measures of the same eternity." And, in *Lolita*, Humbert Humbert points out to his reader that "I substitute time terms for spatial ones."

The spiral offers us an explanation, also, of the *marrowsky* (Nabokov, or rather Charles Kinbote, defines this word in *Pale Fire* as "a rudimentary spoonerism"). A *marrowsky* is, almost, *Makarovski, Macaronski, Skomorovski,* and *Komarov; Kinbote* is *Botkin, Botkine, Bodkin,* and, with a leap, *Nabokov*. To say *Nabokov* is no violation of the truth, for the *marrowsky*, the similarity of word to word, is the marrow of his work. The purpose of this technique is clear. Joan Clements of *Pnin*, as she is speaking of an unnamed author (Nabokov himself?), asks: "But don't you think . . . that what he is trying to do . . . practically in all his novels . . . is . . . to express the fantastic recurrence of certain situations?"[33] Recurrence, indeed, but in a different form. What we perceive is the echo of an inside arc of a spiral by an outside arc; it is a type of relativity. Physical time, says Pnin in his discourse on *Anna Karenin(a)*, is not the same as "spiritual time."

In the poem "An Evening of Russian Poetry," Nabokov says that he speaks of words instead of "*knowledge nicely browned*/ Because all hangs together — shape and sound,/heather and honey, vessel and content." Words are "shells that hold a thimble and the sea."[34] In brief, Nabokov is showing that the world and the language we use to *create* the world are intricately, and inextricably interwoven.

What the artist does is not to recapture just past action, not even past meaning, but to capture, again and again, the *order of the world* in an artistic form. More precisely, art shows the form of and gives form to the world.

The artistic process is a search for correspondences that give structure. The novel, then, offers us a kind of esthetic completeness in itself; by its discovery of forms for the rest of the world, it makes a complete form. A novel, says Nabokov in the epilogue to *Lolita*, is not a social report, not a myth, not an allegory. Still, we must insist that it always has a subject. That subject is form itself, although "form" here means much more than just a pleasingly regular structure.

Now, the world and words *are* involved in time — in something that seems separate from them. However, in *Speak, Memory*, when Nabokov tells the story of one of his butterfly hunts, the boy Nabokov starts across a Russian bog and arrives on the other side. However, he is not in Russia but in Colorado some forty years later. And he says, "I confess I do not believe in time. I like to fold my magic carpet, after use, in such a way as to superimpose one part of the pattern upon another," and then he expresses gratitude "to the contrapuntal genius of human fate . . . " (139). Nabokov is praising timelessness; the purpose, the structure, and the texture of his novels are searches for timelessness, not just for time past, but for all time *now*. Timelessness is unity. Sebastian Knight announces, "The only real number is one, the others are mere repetition." History is *one* because it does repeat itself — with variations.

CHAPTER 2

The Themes: The Short Fiction and the First Novels

I The Short Fiction as an Introduction to the Themes

NABOKOV has published a great many short stories in Russian, in French, and in English (most of which are translations from Russian originals). From these he has made several collections; the first Russian one is *Vozvrashchenie Chorba* (*The Return of Chorb*) in 1930; and his most recent English one is *Tyrants Destroyed and Other Stories* in 1975. Most of the stories are rather conventional narratives ending with a slight surprise; but a few, more experimental stories are as good as his best novels and make Nabokov one of our finest short story writers. But no matter what the original language, the time of composition, or even the value of the individual story, each of his stories is a variant combination of certain of the same elements. Therefore, an examination of a few of them can be one of the most direct ways of arriving at Nabokov's themes. There is, first, his delight in language; for language, of course, is the artist's means for creating a world and preserving it against time. As Andrew Field points out, Nabokov again and again devotes a story to "a character's fixation upon his past"[1]; and the character's concern with time, with the loss of time, is the figure for the artist's concern. There is, second, the continual eruption of the irrational, the ironic, and the paradoxical; for the art work, which gives order to chaos, will not let us forget that chaos threatens us. And, third, despite Nabokov's qualifications, the short stories express a deep concern with the moral life.

We can take as an example of this concern with moral life "The Dashing Fellow," an early and simple Russian story in which a lady-killing Russian meets a woman on a German train and takes her to her home. Momentarily, he is left alone. A messenger arrives, saying that the woman's father is dying and will not live through the night.

The Russian promises to give the woman the message; but, as soon as she returns, he makes love to her while holding her against the table — a quick, nasty act that satisfies only him. Then, pretending that he is leaving to get a cigar, he departs forever. The story is a bitter, moral statement that demonstrates the failure of human feeling on the part of the man.

This sexual theme is only apparently important to an earlier (1926) story, "Skazka" ("A Nursery Tale"). In it, the tone and the point of the story are not bitter but almost sympathetic. The protagonist, the mild little man Erwin, dreams repeatedly of having most of the women he sees; but he is so shy he cannot bring himself to speak to a woman. Then he meets the devil, who comes in the form of a woman named Mrs. Monde. Mrs. Monde grants Erwin his harem with the proviso that he must choose the women in it between noon and midnight on the next day and that the number must be odd. But Erwin, after choosing eleven, sees a young girl whom he must have (a prefiguring of *Lolita*) and so must find a thirteenth. But he unknowingly chooses the first woman he had already chosen that day; and, since his time has expired, he loses them all. Nabokov does not resort, however, to the usual ending since Erwin does not lose his soul; he simply loses the women. As he walks home, tired, he thinks that "tomorrow was Monday and it would be hard to get up."[2] His is a sad little story.

A sadder story and one more of failure — for failure is to be a major Nabokovian subject — is "Lips to Lips" in which a pathetic, talentless émigré who has writing ambitions is tricked into supporting financially a failing magazine in return for which the magazine finally publishes a bit of his novel. By accident, he hears the truth; and the story closes with his anguished attempts at convincing himself that it cannot matter, that he will be recognized as a great writer after his death; but he knows that he will have to continue with financial support for the magazine in order to get more of his work published.

But Nabokov's major themes — that of the past which is both preserved in art and lost in time, and that of the continual threat of the loss of order in chaos — can perhaps be best examined in two rather longer stories: "Spring in Fialta," and "Conversation Piece, 1945." "Wait a moment, where are you leading me, Victor dear," the Nina of "Spring in Fialta" asks the narrator. And he thinks, "Back into the past, back into the past, as I did every time I met her . . . ."[3] He holds her in his memory, trying to comprehend her; for she is part of his life and so of himself: she is, in brief, part of his own identity. This search for identity, for self- knowledge, a search that appears in almost all of Nabokov's fictions, is not only expressed in the concern with lost time but with the figure of the "double." When Nabokov says that "there are no 'real' doubles" in his novels and adds that the subject of the *doppelgänger* "bores" him,[4] we must simply point to the ever-recurring near double, the perhaps "false" double but doubles of a kind nevertheless, which exist and which show us order and disorder at once.

The structure of "Spring in Fialta" most clearly reveals its themes. We can best describe the structure as a series of waves within a circle; but, because the circle is not quite closed, the story is not repeated. This circle, or rather spiral, of time is the present with which the story begins and with which it ends — there is a time passage of less than a day; and the waves are those memories, flashbacks, of the narrator that are interspersed within the present of the story — his recreation of the whole fifteen-year relationship between the woman, Nina, and himself. The narrator, Victor (not too surprisingly Nabokov was almost christened Victor through the misunderstanding of the Russian priest who baptized him), has arrived in the little Italian town of Fialta on a rainy spring day — a Prospero-like misty-rain world which will melt in a dream dissolution at the end of the story, leaving Victor elsewhere. There he meets Nina, a chance meeting as all their meetings have been; and he spends the day in her company.

Nina is the wife of the writer Ferdinand, another of those many writers who echo, shadow, or double one another and their creator. Ferdinand, it is true, seems to have little in common with Nabokov except that he is a "weaver of words," a phrase that Nabokov also uses to describe the much more sympathetic writer-translator Ember of *Bend Sinister*. But, when Victor objects to Ferdinand's puns and "art of verbal invention" and asks why one should write "things that had not really happened in some way or other" (all qualities of Nabokov as artist), we must see another mask of the author, even if a distorted one. Victor himself thinks that only the heart should have imagination and that the writer should "rely upon memory, that long-drawn sunset shadow of one's personal truth" (13 - 14). And, of course, this use of his own memories in his fiction is a Nabokovian characteristic.

But Nabokov's doubles do not bear the meaning of the story, for we must analyze the narrative and the characters to discover it. The "waves" of memory evoke a Nina who is almost the same as she was when she was a girl but who, in each memory, is also subtly different; therefore, time does move. In Victor's first memory, she is seventeen and looks twenty; in this last meeting, she is thirty-two and looks much younger. Time does move, but it also holds still. When Victor speaks of "the Fialta version of Nina" (7), her present double, he also recalls being "introduced" to her twice; and both times her body, as she sits on a couch, has been folded into a "Z." And thus memory, the past, gets involved with the future as well as the present. As Victor, Nina, Ferdinand, and Ferdinand's shady friend Segur pass the automobile that will carry Nina to her death, Victor looks back; "and [he] foresaw, in an almost optical sense," the three getting into that automobile for the death ride; Nina will never grow older (24).

Not only structure and character give doubleness to the story, for the repetition of significant images and words adds to this feature of it. Fialta echoes Yalta, a town from Victor's (and Nabokov's) past; and both echo *fialka*, the Russian word for *violet*, a color and a flower that dance through the story from the first page to the last. We also have the young Italian girl "of twelve or so, with a string of heavy beads around her dusky neck" (2), whose double (or herself) reappears later as "a native child, a swarthy girl with beads around her pretty neck" (18) to receive candy from Ferdinand. And, most expressively, Nabokov uses the circus as an image of death; the recurrent glimpses, poster, advertising parade, and finally the truck of the circus that is coming to Fialta show that the wave of the future cuts across that of the past; for Nina is killed• when the departing automobile crashes into the arriving circus truck.

In "Conversation Piece, 1945," first published as "Double Talk," a title that indicates its theme, the narrator, still another writer, has an actual double: "a disreputable namesake, complete from nickname to surname, a man whom I have never seen in the flesh . . ." (125) but once seen in a photograph. And the reader, who never sees the man either, cannot be certain that the person has a physical existence. Not only do the two share names; they also share an acquaintance with Mrs. Sharp who, naturally-unnaturally, is not one but two Mrs. Sharps: the first is of a leftist political persuasion, the second, a rightist.

Except perhaps for "The Assistant Producer," which has the unreality of the film script that it is in part parodying — paradoxically, that story is based on an actual case of kidnap-murder among the

Russian exiles in Paris — or for "First Love" and "Mademoiselle O" (both of which are really sections of *Speak, Memory*), "Conversation Piece, 1945" is the most "social" of Nabokov's English or "Englished" short stories. The double of the narrator is a "very White *émigré*, of the automatically reactionary type" (126), whereas the unnamed narrator is a liberal who is opposed to the "Communazist state" that Nabokov himself excoriates in his English introduction to *Invitation to a Beheading* (1959) and in *Bend Sinister* (1947). For example, one of the unpleasant characters of "Conversation," a Colonel Melnikov or Malikov (even his name cannot be clear), is able to attack the "Jewish Bolsheviks," emphasizing the adjective; but, although a White Russian, the colonel can happily admire the tyrannous Joseph Stalin, who is for him one of Russia's "three great leaders," along with Ivan the Terrible and Peter the Great (136). The totalitarian nationalism — the state and the society that "save" men from their lonely singleness — appeals to him; but the artistic image is that left and right join and become one if the political circle continues.

The social, political commentary is not, however, the burden of the story, unless it is phrased as the ability of each of us to contain contradictions. For, although the apparent subject is the "conversation" among a group of Nazi sympathizers to which the narrator, mistaken for his double, is invited, the real subject is the narrator and his double, the double talk. Each pursues and is pursued by the other, and both pursuits are unwitting and unwilling. A library demands that the narrator return a copy of the "Protocols of the Wise Men of Zion," a forged piece of anti-Semitic propaganda he would not think of borrowing; he is arrested for breaking mirrors (in which his double no doubt saw him) which he did not break; and, at the end, he gets a letter from his double which begins: "Esteemed Sir. You have been pursuing me all my life" (142). They, too, are two, and yet one: they are *doppelgängerin* obsessed despite their wishes. And once more Nabokov does not neatly resolve his situation — the two will continue to revolve around each other, moths for the other's flame.

II   *The Young Novelist and the Discovery of Themes:*
Mary (Mashenka)

In 1956, Nabokov protested that, since none of his "American friends" had read his Russian books, "every appraisal" limited to his English ones would necessarily be inexact.[5] But the differences lie in the increasing complexity rather than in the basic themes of the books. If *Pale Fire* is difficult, it is because of its structure and not because its attitude is different from that of the very earliest Russian works. Moreover, the themes of the short stories, added to perhaps, reappear: the mystery of time and space; the loss and redemption of the past; and the necessary pursuit of art. And, despite variations, the same stylistic concerns are present: the exact word, the exact image, and the precise use of point of view. Indeed, Nabokov's handling of point of view remains a constant technique in almost all of his works. He uses either the first person or the third person limited; and then, the author's voice, the creator's voice, suddenly directly addresses the reader to remind him that he should not confuse the work of art with something called "reality."

In short, the young Sirin, if not exactly the older Nabokov, is a very close relative; and Sirin is perhaps best described in Nabokov's words:

Among the young writers produced in exile he was the loneliest and most arrogant one. . . . [His] admirers made much, perhaps too much, of his unusual style, brilliant precision, functional imagery and that sort of thing. Russian readers . . . were impressed by the mirror-like angles of his clear but weirdly misleading sentences and by the fact that the real life of his books flowed in his figures of speech, which one critic has compared to "windows giving upon a contiguous world . . . a rolling corollary, the shadow of a train of thought."[6]

But, if the Russian works are not so different from the English ones, the Russian ones do become something different in translation. All of the Russian novels have been translated since Nabokov's 1956 statement; and, although the English versions are not always quite literal and have been "translated" by various hands, Nabokov always supervises and revises; therefore, the English versions are truly his, and are both old and new at the same time. And that is, once more, the Nabokovian paradox — the separateness at the same time that everything is related.

Nabokov's first novel, *Mashenka*, was published in 1926; it was translated "by Michael Glenny in collaboration with the author" and published as *Mary* in 1970. This translation follows the original most literally, as Nabokov notes in his introduction[7] in which we find his insistence on the primacy of the original that affected all his later translations from other authors such as Pushkin's *Eugene Onegin*. As a result, *Mashenka* is nearly *Mary*, and *Mary* can be used as text without doing violence to the original. The faithfulness of translation is not attributable, however, only to a theory of translation; part of it is Nabokov's "attachment to my first book" (even if, paradoxically, in his first version of *Speak, Memory*, then called *Conclusive Evidence*, he says that Sirin's, or his, "first two novels are to my taste mediocre.")[8] *Mashenka* is not an important work, either in Russian or English — it is, in fact, a rather sentimental novel; but it does let us see how Nabokov, from the beginning, defined himself as a writer.

The action of the short novel is deceptively uncomplicated. It covers just one week and takes place in or not too far from a Berlin *pension* run by a Russian émigré woman; and, as Andrew Field has indicated, "the novel is built on the simple and time-honored principle of the Grand Hotel grouping."[9] The protagonist, the tired young émigré, Lev Glebovich Ganin, has been having an affair with the girl Lyudmila — not living in the *pension* — and he wants to escape not only from the affair but from Berlin. However, the novel is also built on another time-honored principle, that of the triangle — a pattern of relationships and action that Nabokov uses in much of his fiction. In the novel's opening scene, Ganin is caught in a stalled elevator with another of the boarders, a garrulous stranger, who tells Ganin that he is expecting his wife to arrive soon from Russia. Before long, Ganin discovers that the wife of this other man, Alfyorov, is his own first and great love, the girl Mary ("Mashenka" in the original).

Ganin's story is very nearly Nabokov's; but the autobiography, transformed into fiction, is no longer autobiography. Nabokov admits in the introduction to *Mary* that there are "certain similarities between my recollections and Ganin's," for Ganin's Mary is "a twin sister" of Nabokov's Tamara, and the two also share a memory for the same estates and landscapes, even of the Oredezh River (xi - xii). Yet even in these similarities exquisite differences exist. In *Speak, Memory*, Nabokov describes "a certain pavilion" on the family estate in which he first spoke to Tamara; and the words are a direct theft (in translation) from his own *Mashenka*. Put side by side, the two descriptions emphasize what has happened: the novel's language (in both Russian and English versions) is richer, perhaps because, as Nabokov himself indicates, Ganin was "three times closer to his past than" (xii) Nabokov was in *Speak, Memory*. But there is, too, the contrast created by the artist's free imagination in the novel and by the restriction imposed on that same artist by the necessity of keeping to "historical" truth in his memoir. Oddly, the past is better recaptured and recreated in the art work.

A goodly portion of the novel is devoted to Ganin's memories, to his attempt to recapture and hold the past. Stirred to life, he now plans to forestall Alfyorov and to meet Mary first; but the girl never actually appears in the novel: she is a name and a memory, but in memory she is most alive. Yet, even though Ganin does get Alfyorov so drunk that he passes out and cannot go to meet his wife, Ganin hesitates, turns away from the station at which Mary is arriving, and leaves the city for the south.

But the real action of the novel occurs in the interweaving of Ganin's memories with the dreary present, Germany in the 1920s, unreal and empty, as experienced by the exiles in the *pension*, these sensitive, artistic, intellectual, and lost people: "It was not simply reminiscence but a life that was much more real," Ganin thinks, recalling his past, forming his past, "much more intense than the life lived by his shadow in Berlin" (55 - 56). The essence, then, of the novel is loss — loss created by this constant interweaving of past time with present time. For instance, a sad comedy exists in the fact that the rooms in the *pension* are marked by leaves torn off a calendar from a past year — and Alfyorov's door is April 1 while Ganin's is April 2 (April 1 is a date that appears again and again in Nabokov's work). In addition, there is the sadness, if not the comedy, of Ganin's actually seeing himself in a past moment: at a movie with Lyudmila and Klara, his fellow boarder, he suddenly remembers that this is a movie in which he appears as an extra. And with shame he suddenly sees "himself," his "*doppelgänger,*" on the screen; but, mixed with his shame, he suddenly has "a sense of the fleeting evanescence of human life" (21 - 22). This shame and this sense of evanescence are the motives for his not meeting Mary; for such a renewal would be something different and could only disappoint. He could not relive the life that he had lived and that still lives in his memory where time has been overcome.

The lives of the other boarders at the *pension* are, also, paradigms of lostness, the past lost and present lost. Even Alfyorov, this foolish, sentimental blockhead, when asked what he did in Russia before his departure, responds: "I don't remember. How can one remember what one was in a past life — an oyster maybe, or a bird, let's say, or perhaps a teacher of mathematics? In any case our old life in Russia seems like something that happened before time began, something metaphysical or whatever you call it . . . metempsychosis" (24 - 25). But there is no real metempsychosis, or transmigration of souls — there is only the death of the old and no assurance of a new life. The old poet, Podtyagin, speaks of his commitment to poetry in terms of

the birch trees that appeared in his poems: "What a fool I was — for
the sake of those birch trees I wasted all my life, I overlooked the
whole of Russia. Now, thank God, I've stopped writing poetry. . . . I
put everything into my poetry that I should have put into my life,
and now it's too late for me to start all over again" (41 - 42). Art is an
illusion if it does not allow life outside itself. And Klara, when asked
by Podtyagin if she loves Russia, suddenly replies, "I'm already
twenty-six . . . I type all morning, and five times a week I work until
six. I get very tired. I'm quite alone in Berlin. What do you think . . .
will it go on like this for long?" (53 - 54). Podtyagin responds, almost
irrelevantly, "I only hope to God I can get to Paris" (54); but he will
not. He obtains an entrance visa from the French; and, after incredible difficulties, he secures an exit visa from the Germans; but, since
he then loses his passport, he will go nowhere.

The irony is that Ganin has two passports. One of them is Russian,
old but genuine; the other, Polish and forged. And his real name is
not Ganin. In short, his present existence is as unreal as Podtyagin's
although he is young and will continue to move. But his real life lies
in his past which is both recoverable and utterly lost. The tension of
this paradox makes the novel, then, more comprehensive than it
would at first seem: it makes the novel, finally, Nabokovian and connects it with all his other works.

III   King, Queen, Knave (Korol', Dama, Valet)

"Of all my novels this bright brute is the gayest," Nabokov says of
his second novel, _Korol', Dama, Valet (King, Queen, Knave)._
"Constructed" in the winter of 1927 - 1928 in Berlin, the novel was
published in 1928.[10] Whatever Nabokov's own mood was in
"constructing" it, and no matter what the novel's tone, its subject
seems a strange one for the novelist, despite his return to the
triangle; for his characters, as well as his setting, are German. The
young German countryman, Franz Bubendorf, arrives in Berlin to
work for his relative, Kurt Dreyer; Dreyer is married to a bored,
younger woman, Martha; and Martha and Franz soon become
lovers. Martha leads Franz into a plot to kill Dreyer in order to gain
their freedom, each other, and Dreyer's money. But both are bumbl-
ing fools, and only at the last do they contrive a functional plan: they
propose to drown Dreyer, who cannot swim. However, when the
three are in the boat, Dreyer casually mentions a business plan by
which he will gain a good deal of money; and the mercenary Martha

delays the killing. Ironically, Martha suddenly falls ill and dies. Yet
the novel is a bright, gay book, not a gloomy study of a stolid German world. It is a more important work than *Mashenka* because of
the gaiety which gives it life, but it lacks the richness and complexity
of Nabokov's major works.

Nabokov claims that, at the time he wrote this novel, he did not
speak German and had almost no real contact, either socially or
culturally, with the German world around him. And yet the
" 'human humidity,' *chelovecheskaya vlazhnost'*," of *Mashenka* was
not what he wished in his new novel (viii). In *Korol', Dama, Valet*,
Nabokov avoided the sentimentality of his first novel; he did not
want to be like Balzac and make a voluminous record of contemporary manners. Nabokov knew the contemporary manners of the
Russian expatriates only too well, and his turning to a German milieu
is, paradoxically, a flight from journalism. But there is evasion in
Nabokov's denial of knowledge of German society; his knowledge of
the contemporary manners of Germany and the United States, for
example, is so exact and extensive that its realization in his novels
contributes greatly to their attractiveness. If he deals, in the end,
with irrationality, it is not by way of romantic vagueness.

Nabokov in fact makes fun of "irrationality" and of himself
through the concrete gaiety of the novel. He speaks of "the god of
chance (Cazelty or Sluch [Russian for "rumor"], or whatever his real
name was)," who can be imagined "in the role of a novelist or a
playwright, as Goldemar [author of a play called *King, Queen,
Knave*] had in his most famous work" (224). But this comic
irrationality is best displayed by sentences that are themselves comic
— and which twist the world: "Her mother had died when Martha
was three — a not unusual arrangement. A first stepmother soon
died too, and that also ran in some families" (65). If these sentences
seem to echo Gertrude Stein, we must respond that they never function as Stein's do — they are an intimate, rational collocation of
irrationalities.

But, always, the "irrational" involves a questioning of
"reality"; it is a way of discovering what the truth behind
appearances might be, or of finding that only appearances exist.
Franz, who is the "knave" of this novel, first sees the "queen,"
Martha, as they ride together on a railroad car; when she leaves, he
reconstructs her in his mind; but he changes her head by replacing it
with "the face of one of those bold-eyed, humid-lipped Berlin

beauties that one encounters mainly in liquor and cigarette adver-
tisements. Only then did the image come to life . . ." (14). She
becomes, in short, commercialized sex and is utterly false.

Much later, after Franz has possessed the woman many times and
after they have considered all the ways they can destroy Dreyer, the
"king," Franz tries, in working on a male mannequin with a "horrible face," to remember where he has seen that face before, and then
"Yes, of course — long, long ago, in the train. In the same train there
had been a beautiful lady wearing a black hat with a little diamond
swallow. Cold, fragrant, madonna-like. He tried to resurrect her
features in his memory but failed to do so" (170). Still later he compares her face to that of a white toad; she changes, in some ten
months, from the utterly inaccessible, almost invisible, goddess to
the animal. But none of his perceptions and none of his memories
have much relationship to the actuality. The woman is neither
goddess nor animal; she is, morally, nearer the toad.

Even the book's gestures towards its literary ancestors are
perversely irrational; it is, in large part, a series of parodies that
suggest that all art is irrational. When Nabokov makes in his novel
his bow toward Tolstoi's *Anna Karenin* (he objects to putting an "a"
at the end of this last name since it is not an English ending) in his
foreword to the English version, or his more than a bow to Flaubert's
Madame Bovary, he indicates his way of pointing out that both are
manipulations of actual life, especially of the bourgeois world and of
world views. Parody is artifice, a way of measuring and overcoming
the actual.

More of Nabokov appears in *King, Queen, Knave* than is immediately apparent: the authorial personality controls our vision and
is a continual reminder that this book is a work of art. And, if the title
is from cards (with another literary allusion to Alexander Pushkin's
"The Queen of Spades"), the English title (but not so much the Russian one) brings in Nabokov's love for chess; the notation in chess for
king, queen, and knight is, we should remember, *k*, *q*, and *kn*. And
the plot of the novel, like that of *The Defence*, his next novel, is an
elaborate chess game, although here, at the end, the queen is
sacrificed, thereby saving the king — or, perhaps, the queen destroys
herself, thereby saving the king. And, ironically, the English "jack"
is not a knight; in this case, he is really a "knave." In brief, another
elaborate play on words indicates themes; but these themes are of
possible, multiple, and sometimes contradictory meanings.

Nor does the novel escape Nabokov's inquiry into time and its relationship to creation. The first words of the English version are about creation and so perhaps creative: "The huge black clock hand is still at rest but is on the point of making its once-a-minute gesture; that resilient jolt will set a whole world in motion" (1). Time does begin, and the world is set in motion; the railroad station, not the train, departs; and the reader is on a train, unmoving, since all movement is relative to us. Only within the train can we perceive our own movement and, therefore, our own time. But all other movements and times are strange and unbelievable.

Franz Bubendorf, the young country-boy, is on his way to the great city where he will be initiated into and corrupted by the bourgeois life. But, as usual with Nabokov, a reversal of the expected pattern occurs: Franz, a rather nasty, insensitive young lout, is not the pure and innocent young countryman. (*Bube* is German for *knave, scamp, jack* in cards; *dorf* is *village*; and so what we have is the village knave.) At the beginning, Franz seems to be more sensitive and innocent than he really is — although the fact that he has no real will of his own does not make him morally attractive. He rides in a third-class car; and the people there — the people of his actual class, ugly, deformed, dirty, smelly — repel him. But this repulsion is largely because he believes that there is another, richer life — a life richer in material things. And so, fleeing his class, railroad and social, he blunders into a second-class car. Relieved, he pays the extra money, although doing so goes against his peasant thriftiness. But this exchange of money which takes Franz higher in the social scale is an underlying theme of the novel — it is about that class which obsessed Balzac, the money-conscious, status-hungry bourgeoisie.

In this second-class car, Franz unknowingly sits in the same compartment with the people he is traveling to Berlin to see: his never-before-glimpsed relative, his mother's cousin, Dreyer, and Dreyer's wife, Martha. The Dreyers are in second-class as a kind of slumming; therefore, Franz's reality, this richness, is to them a glimpse into the lower depths. Franz, seeing these elegant strangers, "mentally" calculates "how many days of his life he would give to possess this woman" (12). He will, of course, possess her; but she never again has the attraction, the beauty, that she has when she seems the mysterious, unavailable, upper-class woman. They, on the other hand, hardly notice him.

In brief, these people have no real existence; they have only a social function — or, if we wish, they have only the function of the

cards that give the novel its name and that are in the end in-
terchangeable. This surface "reality" affects all the characters:
Franz, on his first night in Berlin, accidentally crushes his glasses under his feet; without them, he is almost blind; and the world is a
lovely haze. As a result, he misinterprets the world: setting off for the
Dreyers, floating in a world of rich, vague colors, he hears an angel
singing on the stairs. But that angel, so unseen, so misunderstood, is
only a chambermaid in actuality — but also a human being.

And the meeting with Martha is equally absurd. He can barely see
her and certainly does not recognize her. She does, however, connect
him with the young provincial who had ridden with her and Dreyer
in the train. But her surprise is mild; the wonderful coincidences of
this world and of Nabokov's worlds have little meaning for her since
she has no capacity for wonder. What she does recognize is what she
will be able to do with Franz — the new role she will give him: he is
"warm, healthy young wax that one can manipulate and mold till its
shape suits your pleasure" (31). But, as an artist, Martha is a fraud;
she will create nothing. She is acting out of a convention, not
creating.

Martha is a playing-card character — not because Nabokov
creates one but because her one-dimensionality is an aspect of his
design. Martha is not really unhappy in her marriage since her concept of it is a rigidly conventionalized one. Nonetheless, her conventional view is not that of the German middle class; Martha's is
created, in large part, from the cheap films of the 1920s and is based
on her lower-class idea of what true bourgeois life should be.

Martha's convention includes, not too surprisingly, the possibility
of a lover. However, Martha will not take her lover as Flaubert's
Emma Bovary took hers as the fulfillment of some foolish but
passionate quest for life. Martha will take hers because, even though
she momentarily realizes that she is breaking one kind of a convention, she is nevertheless fulfilling another. She thinks, soon after
meeting Franz, "It must happen sooner or later. It is inevitable"
(56). And therefore she will "strictly adher[e] . . . to every rule of
adultery . . ." (115). But the authorial voice adds, "She was no Emma, and no Anna" (101).

Dreyer, the deceived husband in this absurd triangle, is not quite
so flat, so bare, and so base as Martha or Franz. He approximates
that figure of the artist which Khodasevich has pointed to in Sirin's
work: although Dreyer is a very successful businessman, he is also a
dreamer, a would-be man of action, a man of inventive imagination,

the sensitive man who perceives and recognizes "a Red Admirable butterfly," the reoccurring lepidopteron that is almost Nabokov's heraldic beast. Dreyer is, in short, more human than Franz or Martha — less a playing card. While Franz was riding in his third-class compartment, he had been most repelled by an unfortunate man with no nose and almost no lips. Dreyer, seeing the same man later, is not repelled; he notes instead that the man has "the nose of a baby monkey" (16). Although he too does not quite grant the man human status, he does not withdraw in horror.

Dreyer also has a sense of humor. He is delighted by the fact that he and Martha had ridden facing Franz in the railcar without knowing that they would meet the following day as relatives. What makes the situation humorous for him is that he cannot remember exactly what he and Martha had said on that journey, nor can he guess what Franz might have overheard. Moreover, Dreyer is amused by his house, and by the fact that Martha thinks it is excellent, although "neither aesthetic nor emotional considerations ruled her taste; she simply thought that a reasonably wealthy German businessman . . . ought to have a house exactly of that sort . . ." (35).

But Dreyer has his blind spots, his failures in perceiving reality; he does not understand people nor feel for them. A former mistress has told him, "You can hurt people or humiliate them, you are touched not by the blind man but by his dog" (235). And for him, Franz will always remain his "timid provincial nephew with a banal mind and limited ambitions" — a view that is perhaps true, but not true enough. And Martha, "for more than seven years now, had remained the same distant, thrifty, frigid wife whose beauty would occasionally come alive and welcome him with the paradisal smile he had first fallen in love with" (106). But Martha and Franz will plan to kill him.

Yet, ironically, this fault of Dreyer's is a result of his being a bit of an artist, as the author indicates: "Thus an experienced artist sees only that which is in keeping with his initial concept" (106). But we must not take the authorial voice too seriously since it speaks ironically. Dreyer, the "almost" artist, becomes interested in the work of an inventor who has developed some remarkable robots: they are nearly human. True, Dreyer wishes to use them in his store for advertising purposes, but it is because they are imaginative and strange creations. At the same moment, they are our doubles, even if false doubles; but they do comment upon us, upon Dreyer, Martha, and Franz.

And yet, if Dreyer has other oddnesses that are beyond his occasional insensitivity, they somehow make him more human since
they are presented as a comedy of "reality." He makes mistresses of
two "practically identical vulgar young" sisters (142), Ida and
Isolda, doubles who can hardly be said this time to be anything but
doubles; and Dreyer's affair with them is the reversal of Martha's
with Franz. The comedy is in small things, even in Nabokov's
momentarily letting himself once more into his own novel as the
photographer, "a fellow-skier and teacher of English, Mr. Vivian
Badlook" (153), who photographs Dreyer on a skiing holiday with
Ida and Isolda. When Dreyer returns home from that holiday, barely
missing finding Franz in his own bedroom (a parody of the caught-
lover theme, a reversal of what Nabokov does, about this same time,
in the short story, "An Affair of Honor"), he cries to his wife "in his
best English, 'I half returned from shee-ing!' " (160).

This comedy, played against the serious, parodies the serious,
reduces it, and yet heightens it by making it inhuman. Martha has
long since talked Franz into the notion that they must murder
Dreyer in order to keep his money and continue to live in the fashion
to which she has become accustomed. They cheerfully discuss
Dreyer's removal: "The words 'bullet' and 'poison' began to sound
about as normal as 'bouillon' or 'pullet' . . ." (161). And Martha and
Franz now begin to think of Dreyer as "a stylized playing card, a
heraldic design — and it was this that had to be destroyed" (177).

But the concept that actuality is an artifice is worked out by the
theme not only of cards and robot mannequins but by the theme of
the movies. As I have already suggested, Martha's values are in large
part derived from the film; but Nabokov gives us a more concrete
"symbol." Near Franz's room in Berlin, which Martha has helped
him obtain, a "palace-like affair that . . . would be a movie house"
(48) is being erected. The image reappears until Dreyer, out for a
walk, passes it: there is a "huge picture, advertising the film to be
shown on the opening night, July 15, based on Goldemar's play
King, Queen, Knave. . . ." The display is of "three gigantic
transparent-looking playing cards . . . the King wore a maroon dress-
ing gown, the Knave a red turtleneck sweater, and the Queen a black
bathing suit" (216) — all items of apparel that our three characters
are associated with in some way. At this moment, Dreyer, when he
meets Franz on the street, makes him take him to his room which
Dreyer has not seen — and Martha, who has come to surprise Franz,
is there. She holds the door closed against them; and cheerful

Dreyer, not much surprised at Franz's having a girl, departs, unknowing.

The rest of the novel is one of Nabokov's deliberate parodies of expectations — that man can control his acts, that evil will destroy good, and that evil will be punished. The most parodic parody, though, is that evil *is* punished; for, as I have said, it is Martha who dies. Franz and Martha bet Dreyer that he cannot walk to a distant point faster than they can row there; once there, they assume that he, tired, will want to ride back; and, since he cannot swim, they need only overturn the boat and all will be well. But on the return trip, as we have noted, Dreyer, half-casually, half-bragging, announces that the next day he will be "making a hundred thousand dollars at one stroke" (247). He is obliquely referring to the robot mannequins. Insatiable Martha, scenting more money, does not give Franz the signal; they will wait for another day.

The parody is also of art: in her final illness, Martha perceives herself from the outside, sees herself as her own double — but she has gained no insight. As a bad author, she thinks of how happy she and Franz "had been in the rhythm of that earlier novel in those first chapters . . ." (252). They had been happy, but that earlier novel had never existed. By this time, Franz has long since fallen out of love; and he now conceives himself to have been an honest youth seduced by an older woman who, despite all her external elegance, "resembled a large white toad" (259).

Dreyer, leaving Martha without knowing that she is ill, attends a performance of the robot mannequins, the patent to which he owns and wishes to sell; but the mannequins fail horribly — a mockery of the failure of Martha, Franz, and Dreyer. Afterward, Dreyer returns to find his wife dying. But there is one last irony: Dreyer receives a telegram from the would-be buyer of the mannequins, offering to purchase them for the hundred thousand dollars. When Martha dies, only Dreyer suffers; for Franz is horribly relieved — and the last sound of the book is the sound of his "frenzy of young mirth." The book ends, then, with a parody of gaiety that is gruesomely comic. But this comedy is the only possible defence against the vision of chaos, moral and personal, that the novel has examined.

CHAPTER 3

The Young Man Who
Loses the Game

I The Defense (Zashchita Luzhina)

NABOKOV himself, in his foreword to the English translation, gives most clearly what many readers and critics have
found in his third novel, *Zashchita Luzhina* (*[Luzhin's Defense]*
1930), or, in the English version, *The Defense*, (1964):

> Of all my Russian books, *The Defense* contains and diffuses the greatest
> "warmth" — which may seem odd seeing how supremely abstract chess is
> supposed to be. In point of fact, Luzhin [the chess grandmaster protagonist]
> has been found lovable even by those who understand nothing about chess
> and/or detest all my other books. He is uncouth, unwashed, uncomely —
> but as my gentle young lady (a dear girl in her own right) [Luzhin's wife] so
> quickly notices, there is something in him that transcends both the
> coarseness of his gray flesh and the sterility of his recondite genius.[1]

That Nabokov should be a little sarcastic about the supposed
abstractness of chess, the game which he regards so passionately,
says plainly, if ironically, that the book concerns feeling. And that he
should remark upon Luzhin's lovableness is perhaps surprising,
although it should not be. Once again, if Nabokov rejects the sentimental, he does not reject human emotion.

For Luzhin is a sympathetic character, presented sympathetically.
He is an outsider, the eternal exile, a sufferer. The only child of in-
dulgent, well-off, incompatible parents, he really has no family; and
he almost by chance discovers a reason for living — chess. Taken
over and managed by the rather disreputable Valentinov, Luzhin
spends his adolescence and young manhood doing nothing but play
chess. However, after meeting a young Russian girl and falling in
love with her, he leaves his isolation long enough to ask her to marry
him; and she accepts his proposal. With the marriage, he seems to

have a chance for some happiness; but his obsession with chess can not be denied. After an interval of madness and then recovery under his wife's care, he is so overwhelmed by a vision of the world in which he is playing, and losing, a gigantic chess game against an unknown opponent that he commits suicide.

But the novel is not only about "emotion," the life of the unhappy Luzhin, but about the artist, since Luzhin, with his intricate creativity in playing chess, is another type of the artist. Khodasevich, in indicating this fact, held that *Zashchita Luzhina* was Nabokov's first major work, since "perhaps for the first time he found the basic themes of his work." Luzhin, Khodasevich adds, is a kind of professional; and, "if the artist is a man of talent and not of genius, [professionalism] will, as it were, suck out his human blood, turning him into an automaton which is not adapted to reality and which perishes from contact with it."[2] This observation presents a major theme of the novel. However, the novel does not quite bring the man, Luzhin, together with the theme of professionalism; Luzhin's madness is not fully motivated but is given to us through a series of metaphors. The novel, therefore, is only partially successful because of the conflict between character and theme.

Nabokov attempts to bring together the theme of the failed artist with the character Luzhin by having him search for his own identity, for knowledge of what he is. Luzhin's search for identity is also a search for freedom which is symbolized by the game of chess, by its paradoxes. In chess, a game with exact rules played on a limited field, the number of moves, complications, and patterns is a gesture toward infinity. Luzhin's failure as a person lies in his becoming a prisoner of his art; he is determined by it rather than determining it and himself and thereby making himself free. The true artist is free, even if freedom is the recognition of necessities. Nabokov notes that Luzhin's name "rhymes with 'illusion' if pronounced thickly enough to deepen the 'u' into 'oo'" (7). We must take this seemingly casual remark as not so casual, for Luzhin's life is an illusion — although he himself is not.

In itself almost a chess game, the novel is intended to be a demonstration of its own theme; but, at the same time, it contains the odd, appealing, human Luzhin:

My story was difficult to compose, but I greatly enjoyed taking advantage of this or that image and scene to introduce a fatal pattern into Luzhin's life and to endow the description of a garden, a journey, a sequence of humdrum events, with the semblance of a game of skill, and, especially in the final chapters, with that of a regular chess attack demolishing the innermost elements of the poor fellow's sanity (8).

And so, between the opening lines, with the child Luzhin's suddenly discovering that he is not sure who he is (the reversal of Nabokov's first awareness), to the last line, after he has committed suicide and there is no "Aleksandr Ivanovich" at all, the novel develops in an intricate pattern of flashbacks, of leaps forward, of all times becoming one, of moves that are both artificial and deeply felt.

"What struck him most was the fact that from Monday on he would be Luzhin. His father — the real Luzhin, the elderly Luzhin, the writer of books — left the nursery with a smile . . ." (15). Luzhin has just been told that he will now go to his first school where he will be addressed by this last name that he cannot feel. But he will not fit into that school, just as he does not really fit into his own family — just as he will not fit his new name. And yet, always an outsider, he will unconsciously seek a way to fit. Paradoxically, "the secret for which he strove was simplicity, harmonious simplicity, which can amaze one far more than the most intricate magic" (36). Simplicity, harmonious simplicity, would give him a place in the world. He seems to find what he is seeking in Jules Verne's *Around the World in Eighty Days* or in the adventures of Sherlock Holmes, although "only much later did he clarify in his own mind what it was that had thrilled him so about these two books; it was that exact and relentlessly unfolding pattern . . ." (34).

However, when Luzhin does discover chess, the game, so exact and so patterned, so obsesses him that whatever human contacts he has made or might make are almost completely ignored — a condition that ensures that, if chess fails him, he will fail. In fact, when the Russian revolution sends him into exile, he is not really conscious of what has happened; his life is controlled by chess — and by Valentinov, who delights, for instance, in the fact that Luzhin has denied himself everything, including sex, for chess, since Luzhin makes money but does not know it. Luzhin may be the artist; but he is, in his singlemindedness, both the ideal victim and a slightly inhuman creator.

It is by parodic chance that Luzhin meets his future wife, a daughter of Russian exiles who belong, nevertheless, to a more acceptable world than his: he drops his handkerchief, which is "unusually dirty and had all sorts of pocket debris sticking to it"

(86); and she, walking behind him, picks it up and returns it to him. Now, in his awkward way, Luzhin becomes alive; but he is never really able to talk to her except in strange, dislocated phrases. Still, she does find "something in him"; it is she who recognizes him as "an artist, a great artist. . . . And perhaps it was precisely because she knew nothing at all about chess that chess for her was not simply a parlor game or a pleasant pastime, but a mysterious art equal to all the recognized arts" (88).

His proposal of marriage is as comic as the inverted cliché of their meeting — these almost insane bits of comedy in this comic-tragic novel are the humanizing elements in it; for they are the contrasts that make us aware of the mad absurdity of Luzhin's obsession. Luzhin decides suddenly to leave the hotel where they have met, but he then returns abruptly from the railroad station "on foot — a stout, doleful gentleman, crushed by the heat and in shoes white with dust," pursued by an obnoxious child. He bursts into her room "as if he had butted the door with his head"; and, obviously continuing a conversation he had begun in his head, he cries out, "And therefore in continuance of the above I have to inform you that you will be my wife, I implore you to agree to this, it was absolutely impossible to go away, now everything will be different and wonderful"; and then he suddenly sits down and breaks into tears (102 - 3).

But everything, of course, will not be different and wonderful. Luzhin is still emotionally and intellectually, despite his mastery of chess, a child. He cannot fit into her world; he cannot make the kind of talk, do the kind of things that, even if trivial, are social and human. Therefore, she must become part of his narrow cosmos, even while trying all the time to save him; and their marriage cannot do that. Even as she and he meet, he is preparing for a series of games that will lead him to a confrontation with the Italian master Turati, who becomes, in Luzhin's mind, almost an evil. These games break Luzhin — he does not lose them but becomes physically and mentally ill and has to withdraw with the crucial game undecided. Now Luzhin can think only of chess; the whole world has become chess.

After, as we have noted, Luzhin's wife nurses him back to a kind of health, he does not play chess for a long time. Their life together is, apparently, calm; but Luzhin can never become what he never was. Therefore, the remainder of the novel is a subtle and complex description of Luzhin's decline into complete madness; for chess, taking over the whole world for him, is madness. However, Luzhin is not simply paranoid, for the world accidentally and even deliberately conspires against him. For example, when his wife kisses him, she unconsciously kisses him in the pattern of the knight's move. Luzhin is playing a chess game with an unknown opponent, but the opponent is real since Luzhin's imagination has created a world as real as the "actual." No matter what he does, he cannot discover his opponent's strategy. At last he tries to make a move that the opponent could not foresee, a move that will rescue him from the game and prove his freedom: he leaps from a window, the ultimate gratuitous act. But that too has been foreseen; man cannot escape necessity. As Luzhin falls, he sees only a gigantic chessboard on which he will have to play an eternal, horrible game. The story and the structure come together in his death; his life closes with the chess game he has finished with, as Nabokov himself says, his "suicide, or rather sui-mate . . ." (8).

The themes and the structure of the novel are, then, contained in the first and last lines. In the first line, the young boy discovers that he will now be Luzhin and yet knows that he is not Luzhin; in the last line, where we discover that his first name and patronymic were Aleksandr Ivanovich but that no one, including himself, ever used it we see that he had no real existence and that the shape and the story are his search for existence, which was an escape from absolute necessity. But this statement does not mean that the man, the physical body, does not exist; it does mean that he has had no place in the world as chessplayer, as lover, or as husband. Luzhin's is a very sad story.

II   Glory (Podvig)

In 1930, *Soglyadatay* (*The Spy*, translated as *The Eye*) appeared. This fourth novel, really a novella, is a minor work about the pitiful, failure-prone young Smurov. Smurov, insulted, commits suicide, or at least believes he does; he recovers to lead a life that, to him, is not real since, as he goes along, he is creating both it and an alter ego — in the form of a man of strength and action. When his dream world collapses at the end, he is still denying reality. This story of the man who is trying to recreate his life is not, however, fully developed; and Nabokov, in his next novel, *Podvig* (translated as *Glory*), once more takes up the theme.

When Martin Edelweiss, the protagonist of *Glory*, arrives in London as an exile from his native Russia, he recognizes "certain things" during the evening walk he makes for the first time into the city; for he has already experienced that sensation and sight in his reading, in his imagination, and, most important, in his daydreams. In his daydreams, he had already arrived; he had left his baggage and had walked the streets looking for "Isabel, Nina, Margaret"; and, finding her, he had spent the night with her: "She would not accept his money, she would be tender, and in the morning she would not want to let him go." In reality, he finds the girl; and, although her name is a proletarian Bess, she will not accept money; she responds that, if he wishes, he can take her to a fine restaurant on the next day. But, as he sleeps, she gets up, dresses, and steals ten pounds from his billfold.[3] The dream of love, of power, and of communion becomes not even a commercial transaction with full awareness on both sides but a game of deceit, of appearances that do not match realities — in short, a dream.

The episode is the image of the novel; for Martin is, like his predecessors, a near-artist, the fantasizer whose structures do not quite create nor discover realities. Once again, therefore, Nabokov has examined that odd and ambiguous relationship between the artistic and the practical act. When Nabokov in his introduction to the English version remarks that, of the heroes of his Russian books, "Martin is the kindest, uprightest, and most touching" (xi), he also adds that, to the "gifts" he gave Martin, he deliberately did not give him talent. Although he gave Martin the sensitivity of the artist, he intentionally did not want him to find "in art — not an 'escape' . . . but relief from the itch of being!" (xiii). Martin's need to "be," to create himself if nothing else is, therefore, the subject matter of the novel; and, if his life story has a similarity to that of his creator, we are hardly surprised. Nabokov does ask the reader not to leaf through *Speak, Memory* seeking the similarities, for "the fun of *Glory* is elsewhere" (xiv). The fun of *Glory* is elsewhere, but some of its meanings are contained in its relationship with *Speak, Memory*; the novel is an anti-*Speak, Memory* that demonstrates how one does *not* become an artist.

Martin, like Luzhin, is the son of a well-off Russian family. Reared in St. Petersburg, his childhood life is that of the privileged young of the privileged classes of Russia who indulge in journeys to Biarritz, luxury trains, foreign governesses, and Anglophilism (at least among certain members of the upper classes, such as the Nabokovs). But Martin's parents separate, and then their whole world falls apart as a result of the Revolution. The Edelweisses, mother and son, flee south to Yalta; and there they hear of the death of the father. With the fall of the Crimea to the Communists, the Edelweisses escape in

April, 1919, on board a Canadian freighter — at the same moment, the Nabokovs were actually leaving on a Greek freighter. After stopping in Greece, the Edelweisses settle in Switzerland; and then Martin goes to Cambridge University to complete his education. He meets Sonia Zilanov, daughter of a Russian family, and almost immediately falls in love with her. But she does not love him in return; and, at the last, he sets off on a trip back into Russia, perhaps to cause her to love him, certainly to impress her. With this perhaps fatal gesture, the book ends.

The novel is called, in Russian, *Podvig*; the word, and therefore the title, has usually been translated as *The Exploit*; but Nabokov suggests that it is perhaps better translated as "gallant feat" or as "high deed." Its working title, he says, was *Romanticheskiy vek*, "romantic times . . . because the purpose of my novel . . . lay in stressing the thrill and the glamour that my young expatriate finds in the most ordinary pleasures as well as in the seemingly meaningless adventures of a lonely life" (x). And so, when the novel was translated by his son, Dmitri (in collaboration with Nabokov, of course), Nabokov, wishing to avoid any possibility of a reader's finding the verb "utilize" in the title, decided to change it to "glory" in order to keep "the *podvig*, the inutile deed of renown" (xii). The novel is aimed at the final action of Martin, his departure on his pointless and almost suicidal return into Russia, not to perform an act against the Soviet state but simply to act, to do something without real point. His is a gratuitous act that is quixotic, romantic, self-destructive, and not really self-creative.

However, the novel's plot is hardly a single action; it is much less organized than any of the other early novels of Nabokov because the intrusion of the author's own life upsets the fictional pattern. It is, in short, probably the weakest of Nabokov's longer works; for it is directed, when it has direction, only toward the ending. Structurally, there are the usual experiments with point of view, with time, and with flashback and flash-forward that suggest that reality is paradoxical; but the experiments do not hold the novel together. At best, the novel is a fairy story consisting of a series of fairy stories, none of them well integrated into a realistic world. That Martin Edelweiss' paternal grandfather should have been a Swiss who was the tutor to a St. Petersburg family called Indrikov and who married one of the daughters (1) is certainly acceptable; but the name Edelweiss, this "noble white," joined with the Russian "indrik," which means "unicorn," immediately establishes a world of unrealities that work at cross purposes.

Over Martin's childhood bed hangs a watercolor which images a path winding away into a deep forest. In the English books that his mother, a confirmed Anglophile, read to him in his youth, there was a story about a picture like this one; and the boy hero of the story one night entered the picture and vanished down its path. Later, when Martin remembers this episode, he wonders "if one night he [himself] had not actually hopped from bed to picture, and if this had not been the beginning of the journey, full of joy and anguish, into which his whole life had turned" (4 - 5). He does enter the picture, although only in the sense of an image; at the end of the novel, his English friend Darwin has just informed Martin's mother of her son's disappearance; then, walking away from her house, he starts back to the local Swiss village on a path through the forest; and there "the dark path passed between the tree trunks in picturesque and mysterious windings" (205).

Between these two images lie Martin's wanderings, some like fairy-tales, others nakedly realistic; and there is always the unresolved tension between the two. There are, however, other doublenesses in the novel that are more fruitful, more related to the themes. For instance, all his life Martin has been aware of a kind of split in his character — the possibility that he was a physical coward, despite his courage. His life is a continual examination and testing of himself in order to see if he can face the finality of death, that death symbolized by his stepping through the picture and onto the path leading into the forest.

Even in his relationships with others, this doubleness appears. In Greece, he experiences his first affair with a young married woman named Alla Chernosvitov; she is a second-rate poet, a predecessor of the Liza Bogolepov of *Pnin*, and almost as insensitive and as self-centered. But Martin too is insensitive and self-centered, although he believes himself to feel intensely; for him, Alla is an object, just as the "Isabel, Nina, Margaret" of his dream of London is of an object, not of a real person. Despite Nabokov's assertions, Martin does lack sensitivities toward other people, and this lack is a sign of his failure as artist-figure. On the other hand, at Cambridge, where Martin falls in love with Russia and attempts to recapture its essence, particularly through its literature, until "at last, the voices of the Russian muses began to sound in complete purity" (98), we see his other side. There, too, he makes some close friends, an act that requires some considerable giving of self. This attempt to recover lost Russia is Martin's reality, but it becomes a dream Russia. It will certainly be a major element in his later fantasy of "Zoorland," the northern coun-

try he and Sonia will invent (his Zoorland will never have the solidity
of Nabokov's Zembla in *Pale Fire*, a fantastic land that becomes
quite real *in art*).

But Martin tries to impress his friend Darwin by expanding on his
own life story and by creating a fictional past a little like Smurov's,
but, when he discovers that Darwin's life has been much more ac-
tive, violent, and true, Martin reverses the patterns once again. Even
Sonia is ambiguous — as Nabokov himself admits, she is "a moody
and ruthless flirt" (xi). That is, she will not reveal herself. She plays
with Darwin, getting him to fall in love with her; she leads him —
and Martin — to believe that she returns that love; and then she
laughingly refuses Darwin's proposal. Martin then picks a fight with
Darwin, both as an expression of his jealousy and as an element in his
need to define himself through action since he cannot define himself
as an artist; but, of course, the action is for no purpose.

After his graduation, Martin goes to Berlin, following after the
Zilanovs who have moved there. He makes his living by teaching
tennis (as Nabokov did), and, he also meets the Russian émigrés, the
intellectuals of all sorts that formed Nabokov's world during his
Berlin years. One of the émigrés is the writer Bubnov, who is certainly not Nabokov but who is the one with whom Sonia apparently
falls in love. Among Bubnov's novels is one about a Russian who accompanies Columbus on his journey of discovery — a Columbus
that Martin himself has already thought about in recalling the story
that Columbus went to Iceland to get information from the sailors
there before he set off on his epochal journey westward. "I, too,"
Martin says, "plan to explore a distant land" (128). The land Martin
later explores, the actual Russia, becomes in his and Sonia's rather
adolescent mythmaking imaginations Zoorland, the northern land
that may look forward to the Zembla of *Pale Fire* but even more to
the ugly Ekwilist state of the dictator Paduk in *Bend Sinister*. In
Zoorland everything is equal; everyone is equal, including, for example, physicians who are ordered "to treat all illnesses in exactly the
same way" (148). But this reduction of any world, any state, to a
pure allegory has its terrible dangers if the "reduction" is not
redeemed by the shaping and vital imagination of the mature artist.
Martin's fault is that while not regarding Zoorland as a true picture
of Russia, he begins to act as though it might be. That is, he confuses
levels of reality.

He now becomes his own Columbus, but he prepares himself by
going in a reverse direction; in the south of France, he impulsively

leaves his train, thinking that he has just seen the same lights that he had once seen in his childhood, lights that signified a fairyland merely glimpsed from the speeding train. And so he goes, on foot and in "disguise," to the tiny village of Molignac, the place of the "lights," where he lives as a common laborer, almost free, and momentarily considers giving up his journey into Zoorland. For, if he is playing a role here, he is not trying to impress anyone with it.

But he must write to Sonia to ask her to join him, for he thinks that, if she will come, he can escape his fate; he will be able to settle into the reality of this southern fairy tale. But she refuses him, and he boards the train again for the north. As he goes past the distant lights, he asks the conductor what the lights are: "that's Molignac, isn't it?" And the conductor replies that Molignac can't be seen from the train (166). The conductor is not lying, but he speaks out of ignorance, for Martin has seen the train's lights from Molignac; the confusion of "reality" and "fairy tale" is the confusion of truth.

Now, though, he finds in a Russian émigré paper a story called "Zoorland" that is signed by Bubnov: and he knows that his and Sonia's imaginary and private world has been given to the larger world. But Martin also recognizes that Sonia has betrayed him by talking with someone else about their most intimate communions. He cannot now turn back if he is to create himself. Nevertheless, when, in Switzerland, he makes the acquaintance of Gruzinov — the mysterious man of real action, the man who has gone again and again into that mystery which is modern Russia — Martin cannot accept what Gruzinov gives him; for Gruzinov regards Martin's plan, which Martin typically says is someone else's, as ineffably childish.

Then, passing through Berlin, Martin meets Sonia for the last time — and also Darwin who is engaged to be married to an English girl and who does not remember, or is not concerned enough to recall, their past adventures at Cambridge. Not even the past can be shared. Therefore, giving letters addressed to his mother to Darwin who will mail one each week, Martin disappears, going off on his exploit. His is, truly, a romantic act; but it is, in the end, the final confusion of the Zoorland myth — the leap into the picture, into the reality of Soviet Russia — and his exploit can only end fatally. When Darwin goes to Switzerland to inform Martin's mother of her son's action, Darwin momentarily becomes Martin; and he walks into the picture along the path leading into the forest, into a world of pure act and pure absurdity; for the split world cannot be made one.

CHAPTER 4

The Dream Novels of the Mature Artist

I Laughter in the Dark (Kamera Obskura)

NABOKOV'S sixth novel, written in 1931 and published in 1932 as *Kamera Obskura*, was first translated into English and published in London as *Camera Obscura*. Nabokov then retranslated it, with massive changes, as *Laughter in the Dark*, and it was published in the United States in 1938. The book opens with the following passage: "Once upon a time there lived in Berlin, Germany, a man called Albinus. He was rich, respectable, happy; one day he abandoned his wife for the sake of a youthful mistress; he loved; was not loved; and his life ended in disaster.

"This is the whole of the story and we might have left it at that had there not been profit and pleasure in the telling; and although there is plenty of space on a gravestone to contain, bound in moss, the abridged version of a man's life, detail is always welcome."[1] In all its versions, the novel is, like *Despair*, one more retelling of the triangle story; but this novel more nearly follows the classic pattern since the deceived husband (in this case, "lover") does suffer — he does not escape by simply losing an unfaithful wife in the manner Kurt Dreyer does. Yet, as Nabokov's beginning suggests, *Laughter* is not merely about the triangle — it is about art and about the way art is related to life and yet is utterly different.

The Russian original locates the characters in time and place: "In about the year 1925 there spread around the world an endearing, amusing being which has been almost forgotten," a cartoon character, a guinea pig, called Cheepy — Nabokov spells the name with Latin letters the first time it is given in order to supply the English overtones. And, later, "In the beginning of 1928, in Berlin, the art critic Bruno Krechmar" is involved in a law suit over the use of Cheepy in an advertisement for a lipstick.[2]

But the last English version begins with this parody of the standard opening of the English fairy tale, and if, as Dabney Stuart believes, for Nabokov "any fiction is a parody of life,"[3] then we are being given a double level of parody, a parody of a parody. Actually, of course, Nabokov's parodies are deliberate complexities as well as devices for tonal control and for statements of "meaning." If the Russian original is more socially circumstantial, the English opening announces that we are not to be given some naturalist photograph; in fact, the age is alluded to, in this English version, only by one passing mention of Mussolini.

At first glance, the English version seems, however, to be asking the reader not to take the action too seriously since fairy tales are not really serious in themselves. We are assured that, as in most folk tales, there will be no difficulty in recognizing good and evil. But this beginning is a double joke: the real story is yet to be told, and the reader must be aware of being "tricked" by the joke. The author has already entered the book, using the omniscient point of view, not for purposes of self-expression, but in order to make certain that both he and his reader never forget that art is not just a story with an abstractable and presumably more important meaning but rather a tangled web that practices to deceive even when it does not.

There is, however, a fascinating story. Nabokov's statement that "my weakest [novel] is certainly *Laughter in the Dark*"[4] suggests that he ignores both the story and the complexity of its meaning. The story in *Laughter in the Dark* is simpler than that in *Kamera Obskura*, but the stories are basically the same. Albert Albinus — Bruno Krechmar in Russian; Bruno Kretschmar in the first English version — is an art critic who is rich, knowledgeable, and obtuse. These name changes have their significances: they change from dark (Bruno) to white (Albinus) in this shift of languages — and the name Kretschmar, Nabokov admits in *Speak, Memory,* is his way of directly inserting himself into the novel; for it was the name of a German lepidopterist who first described a butterfly that Nabokov mistakenly thought he had discovered.

Albinus is happily married to his wife Elizabeth; has one daughter, the child Irma; and a fat brother-in-law, Paul — all in all, a good solid German family (there are no Russians in this novel). But, although Albinus rather likes his wife and worships his daughter, he is sexually unsatisfied. And so, when by chance he enters a movie theater and sees the young usherette, Margot, he almost immediately falls madly in love. Margot, who has film ambitions, thinks of Albinus as her escape from the life she has been leading into another, higher sphere. She, of course, does not take long to make up her mind about him, although she makes him wait. In fact, she does not allow him to make love to her until she has, half deliberately and half by chance, let Elizabeth know about her and Albinus.

Elizabeth, in a state of shock, leaves, taking the child. Margot and Albinus live together; and Albinus is her fascinated, doting victim. But into their lives comes her first lover, Axel Rex, who had seduced and left her before she ever met Albinus (Rex, in the original Russian, is called Robert Gorn, a name which appears twice in Nabokov's *Pnin* as two different but pleasant Robert Horns — the Russians are likely to pronounce and spell Teutonic names beginning with "H" as "G": Gamlet, Gitler. Nabokov's worlds are connected). Rex is one more "almost" artist who is talented, unsuccessful, utterly dishonest — and his essential falsity denies him the true artistic gift. But, unlike Hermann Karlovich of *Despair*, for instance, Axel Rex knows he is dishonest.

Margot has never forgotten Rex, whom she loves insofar as she can love anyone. And he is fond of her, despite or because of his peculiarities — he is a sly sadist who "as a child . . . poured oil over live mice, set fire to them and watched them dart about for a few seconds like flaming meteors" (142). The authorial voice comments that "their mutual passion was based on a profound affinity of souls" (184). The two resume their affair, thus betraying the betrayer; for Rex, to hide his involvement with Margot, pretends to Albinus to be a homosexual. But Rex is "useful" to Albinus; for Albinus has had an idea, borrowed from the novelist, Udo Conrad, about making little films, "colored animated drawings," which would bring famous paintings to life: Rex is his artistic collaborator. The project hardly advances, however, for the three of them are too preoccupied with their distorted love affair. Albinus lives through Margot; and Margot and Rex live on Albinus.

After the death of his daughter, Albinus begins to feel some kind of guilt: he "was perfectly conscious of the thin, slimy layer of turpitude which had settled on his life" (177). But he cannot leave Margot. He even finances a film in which she can have a part. She is an utter failure as an actress, recognizing the truth herself. Her art can only be in her life, which is corrupt. To save her future, she demands that Albinus get a divorce and marry her; he says he will; but, thinking that he will not, as recompense, offers her a trip.

But Rex, this pretended homosexual with clownlike red lips and white cheeks, comes with them as chauffeur. Everything about them is a parody of life, of love, of domesticity. In the south of France, in Rouginard, they find a hotel with two bedrooms that share a bath; here Rex and Margot can make love while she pretends to be bathing. But here, too, they meet Albinus' novelist friend, Udo Conrad. Unaware of Albinus' and Margot's relationship, Conrad reveals that Margot and Rex are lovers. Albinus drags Margot away in their car; on a winding road he misses a curve, and he is blinded in the crash. The rest of the novel is the description of his slow destruction at the hands of the sadistic Margot and Rex; for Rex, unknown to the blind Albinus, rejoins them in Switzerland where Albinus has taken a house. The terrible pair mock him and bait him; but he cannot respond. He thinks those strange sounds in the air are his imagination and that only Margot, Margot become kind, is with him.

Finally, though, Albinus' brother-in-law, Paul, who has grown suspicious because Albinus' money is being rapidly withdrawn from the bank they share, goes to Switzerland. Discovering the truth, Paul rescues Albinus — and lets Albinus know how he has been treated by Rex and Margot. In Berlin, Albinus is housed at his wife's place; and she, filled with pity, takes care of him. But when he learns by accident that Margot has returned to their former apartment to rifle it, Albinus goes there, taking along a pistol he has carried with him for a very long time — he has fantasized shooting Margot since the very first time he saw her (13). Stumbling into the room, he hears her speak; for she, not looking up, thinks he is the houseporter. But then, seeing him, she moves silently, until she can grapple with the blind man; and in the struggle Albinus is shot and killed: "He sat on the floor with bowed head, then bent slowly forward and fell, like a big, soft doll, to one side" (292).

The book ends, not with a parody of the fairy story, but with a parody of the movie, an art form and business that is both controlling image and controlling theme of the novel:

Stage-directions for last silent scene: door — wide open. Table — thrust away from it. Carpet — bulging up at table foot in a frozen wave. Chair — lying close by dead body of man in a purplish brown suit and felt slippers. Automatic pistol not visible. It is under him. Cabinet where the miniatures had been — empty. On the other (small) table, on which ages ago a porcelain ballet-dancer stood (later transferred to another room) lies a woman's glove, black outside, white inside. By the striped sofa stands a

smart little trunk, with a colored label still adhering to it: "Rouginard, Hôtel Britannia."
The door leading from the hall to the landing is wide open, too. (292)

But these parodies of art forms are not simple literary parodies. They are, rather, parodies of human expectations, of the characters' hopes, of the readers' clichéd reactions, and all are shocks to make us aware. For, if the titles of the various versions of the novel are all references to photographic or moviehouse images, they are also references to our world: the movie is a symbol, but a savage one. Albinus, an obvious fool so far as art is concerned, believes that, "if our age is interested in social problems, there's no reason why authors of talent should not try to help" (216). But Nabokov is not using Albinus to satirize human problems: the book is about those problems. Albinus here is a fool because he thinks of art only as a handmaiden of social change.

What Nabokov is doing is to *use* art himself, but in his own peculiar way. The artist, of course, is the center of the novel: Udo Conrad, "not the famous Pole" (7) (one more famous writer for whom Nabokov has no great regard), is nearly the true artist; and he is set against Axel Rex, the man of talent but not a genius. Rex is an artist of his life; and, not too surprisingly, parodistically, he almost shares ideas about the function of art with Nabokov: "In my opinion, an artist must let himself be guided solely by his sense of beauty: that will never deceive him." But beauty alone is inhuman; and Rex's concept of life as a play, with a stage manager who is "neither God nor the devil," is a snare for the unwary: "The stage manager whom Rex had in view was an elusive, double, triple, self-reflecting, magic Proteus of a phantom, the shadow of many-colored glass balls flying in a curve, the ghost of a juggler on a shimmering curtain. . . ." This imagery is quintessentially Nabokovian, but the implication is not, for "perhaps the only real thing about" Rex is "his innate conviction that everything that had ever been created in the domain of art, science or sentiment, was only a more or less clever trick" (181 - 83).

Udo Conrad, on the other hand, is the man whose only interest is his art, his images, his languages. Asked by Albinus what he is doing in France, his answer suggests that he is an exile from Germany (as Nabokov was from Russia) and that "I'd gladly write in French, but I'm loath to part with the experience and riches amassed in the course of my handling of our language" (215). Conrad is a limited man; he has no life outside his art, and his art is narrow; but he does not deny his calling, and he will not use it to play games with life. And, finally, these parodies of art forms are also shapes of the novel, the form that shows how art is our way of organizing time and of overcoming time. Outside the cinema in which Albinus first sees Margot, a poster portrays "a man looking up at a window framing a child in a nightshirt" (19 - 20). Albinus looks at that poster and then buys the ticket that eventually brings about his death. But the poster also looks ahead, ironically, to the illness of Irma — and to her death. Separated from her father by his own act, she longs for him; getting up from her sickbed, she opens the window to the winter night and sees a man "standing, gazing up at the house" (159). But he is not her father; and, though the image is repeated "by art," the point is that life does not connect so simply.

On the other hand, Albinus comes in at the end of the film and sees "a girl . . . receding among tumbled furniture before a masked man with a gun" (20). This prefigures, and reverses, the final moment when Margot dodges the blind man with his powerless gun. And the authorial voice tells us of the connection when Albinus, returning the second time to the theater in response to his beginning obsession with Margot, thinks that "Any normal man would know what to do"; and the author adds, "A car was spinning down a smooth road with hairpin turns between cliff and abyss" (22) — the image of Albinus and Margot racing away from the hotel on the day after he has learned about her and Rex. The beginning, in brief, is connected with the end, not just because of necessity, but because of artifice; for we might almost say that Nabokov subjugates materiality to the shaping imagination.

The parody thus becomes an element of structure; once more Nabokov is making use of the spiral, that repetition of pattern that is both the same and different. The movie is unreal, life is real, but they are one and the same at the same moment that the one is a commentary on the other and both are commentaries on our "reality."

This sort of doubleness is made part of the novel in the names of Udo Conrad's two books. The first is the *Memoirs of a Forgetful Man*, a delightful monster which parodies a yet unwritten book, *Speak, Memory*; the title, taken seriously, suggests an impossibility that nevertheless exists. The second is *The Vanishing Trick*, "about the old conjuror who spirited himself away at his farewell performance" (7). Albinus speaks of the first chapter of this book to guests at one of his and Margot's parties as one "which, as a matter of fact, he [Conrad] read here, at this table — I mean — well — at a similar table, and . . ." he breaks off; for that table *is* this table (133). Nabokov's art, then, parodies life; but, in so doing, it tells us that people, ambiguous as they are, exist; and that the greatest value is human love.

II   Despair (Otchayanie)

The writing and translating history of *Otchayanie* (*Despair*) is among the most complicated of that of Nabokov's novels — a history that is important because it is intimately involved with his making himself into an English writer. The novel was first composed in Russian in 1932 while Nabokov was living in Berlin; it was serialized in *Sovremennye Zapiski* in Paris in 1934, and published as a book in 1936. At the end of 1936, Nabokov translated the novel into English for a London publisher: "this was my first serious attempt . . . to use English for what may be loosely termed an artistic purpose." He was not pleased with the translation; and he asked "a rather grumpy Englishman" to look at it. The man read only a part, saying that "he disapproved of the book; I suspect he wondered if it might not have been a true confession."[5] This English version was published in 1937, but most of the stock was later destroyed by a bomb — in brief, the novel was not a success. The 1966 English edition is, therefore, almost a new novel. Not only has the translation been revised, but particulars of the original have been changed. However, since the changes do not substantially modify the novel's themes (the second English version does suggest more strongly than the Russian one that the "double" of the protagonist may be a pure projection of the protagonist), we can concentrate on the English edition.

Nabokov's English foreword asserts once more that his novel, "in kinship with the rest of my books, has no social comment to make, no message to bring in its teeth. It does not uplift the spiritual organ of man, nor does it show humanity the right exit" (8). Ignoring the nice gibe at the "spiritual organ," we must assert in response that the novel does have a moral; it does tell us how we should act in the world. If the novel is not quite as successful as some later novels, it is because the mad protagonist, Hermann Karlovich, is a bit too despicable; the theme of the artist does not quite relate to the moral theme. Yet Hermann is interesting, and so is the novel.

Nabokov develops his moral theme by returning to the subject of the double, although this double he calls "false"; and we must

remember that he says that "there are no 'real' doubles in my novels." When Hermann Karlovich, who narrates his own story, begins to think of possible titles for the "confession" he is writing, he considers "The Double," and then adds, "But Russian literature possessed one already. 'Crime and Pun'? Not bad — a little crude, though" (211). And, at another moment, he coins the name "Rascalnikov" (199), making the English "rascal" a part of the name of Dostoevsky's penitent murderer in *Crime and Punishment*. All these are elements of Nabokov's continuing attacks on Dostoevsky — whom he regards as sadly overrated — and also an acknowledgment of thematic relationships since the Dostoevskian note, despite Nabokov's protests, sounds throughout Nabokov's works. Hermann, though, is no "double" of Raskolnokov; he is thoroughly impenitent.

Chronologically, the novel is the tale of Hermann Karlovich, a Russian-born descendant of Baltic Germans — he is given no last name, a significant touch. As the book opens, "the ninth of May 1930" (14), we find him in Prague on a business trip; he is the owner of an almost bankrupt (a fact he keeps hidden from his reader) Berlin chocolate business; and he is trying to save himself. In Prague, he stumbles by chance onto a bum named Felix Wohlfahrt (213) — sometimes these names are too easy: this "Happy" or "Fortunate" is both unhappy and unfortunate, and he does not "fare well."

Hermann Karlovich is overwhelmed with the shock of recognition; for Felix, unshaven and dirty, is his twin: "Is it . . . a crime . . . for two people to be as alike as two drops of blood?" (28). A deliberate irony exists in this rewriting of a Russian cliché, "as alike 'as two drops of water,' " for a bloody murder occurs because two drops of blood are neither that separate nor that alike. The nice touch is that Felix is Hermann's *mirror* image: Felix is left-handed; Hermann, right-handed. Enantiomorphs are not quite doubles; but, as we will discover, Felix is not really Hermann's double.

Hermann's plan and his act are simple enough. He proposes to murder Felix; substitute Felix's "identical" body for his own; disappear; and, then, having his wife Lydia collect his life insurance and join him, live happily ever after. But Hermann also lacks insight; he believes that Lydia loves him — or he at least insists repetitiously that she does. At the same moment, however, he describes their relationship with a cousin of Lydia's, the painter Ardalion, with such exactness that he reveals to the reader that Lydia and Ardalion are having a love affair. He does not know that, even if he had succeeded in his murder plan, she would have betrayed him

to the police. Of course, Hermann may know about Ardalion and Lydia, but he does not tell us since doing so would be a confession he cannot make — it would be a true admission.

Nevertheless, Hermann acts as if he believes in her. He surreptitiously gets Felix to come to Berlin; then, tricking Felix into changing clothes with him, he shoots the man. The murder accomplished, he flees to France, taking on Felix's identity. But he has made two mistakes: he has thought that he and Felix were doubles; but they were so only to his eyes; and he has left Felix's stick behind in the murder car, and the stick has Felix's name on it. The book closes with Hermann's awareness of his error in leaving the stick behind — and with the French police entering the door below his window.

The theme of the "false" double is interwoven with the permanent theme of the artist in a subtle counterpoint in order to demonstrate the function and the power of art. At one moment, Ardalion — a better painter than his "friend" Hermann will acknowledge — insists "that what the artist perceives is, primarily, the *difference* between things. It is the vulgar who note their resemblance." When Hermann answers, "But you must concede . . . that sometimes it is the resemblance that matters," Ardalion retorts, "When buying a second candlestick" (51). Hermann's idea of "resemblance" makes "resemblance" the opposite of Nabokov's idea of "relationships"; Hermann wants actual copies, not the connection made by art. In this sense, he shares the world view of the Ekwilists of *Bend Sinister*, the Zoorlandians, and the Russian Communists — at least as Nabokov views them. Hermann, though a "German" and a businessman, believes in Communism which, he thinks, will result in "Genuine Consciousness," a phrase betrayed by its own capitals. And, in that final classless world, where consciousness will no longer be the product of class, "I visualize a new world, where all men will resemble one another as Hermann and Felix did; a world of Helixes and Fermanns; a world where the worker fallen dead at the feet of his machine will be at once replaced by his perfect double smiling the serene smile of perfect socialism" (169). A man who conceives this state of affairs cannot perceive differences; he cannot perceive.

And so the artist — not Ardalion, but Hermann — is, in *Despair*, one more example of the failed artist, even though he believes this time that he is successful. To him, it is his audience that has always failed: he sees himself as the creator who, perceiving an irrational pattern in reality, takes advantage of that pattern and, by imposing

his will upon pattern and reality, makes them something more. For Hermann believes that he, having been given the perfect other, an identity which is not his, can use that other to commit, to create, the perfect crime. He will deny any existence, though, to his copy; for to one who accepts such copies, only he himself matters.

As for Hermann's ability as an artist, he himself asserts in the very first line: "If I were not perfectly sure of my power to write and of my marvelous ability to express ideas with the utmost grace and vividness . . ." (13), he would not begin. But then he does not quite know how to begin. When Khodasevich asserts that Hermann is a "genuine, self-critical artist" who fails because of a single slip and because he is a man of talent and not of genius,[6] he is only partially correct. Hermann is not a genuine artist solely because he is committed to art; above all, he is not self-critical.

Yet, paradoxically, Hermann does begin; he does write the book; but this "fact" only emphasizes the tension between creative character and creator, Nabokov. This tension is best exemplified by Nabokov's use of point of view; except for *The Eye*, Nabokov makes use of the first person for the first time in a novel. The fictional confession seems limited: the author can only speak through the mind and knowledge of his mouthpiece. But this limitation is only apparent in *Despair*: for Nabokov's authorial personality is behind Hermann's and is forcing Hermann to show himself forth in his true light. It is Nabokov who causes Hermann to report things he is unaware of, to give us insights that he himself does not have. Therefore, if Hermann Karlovich does exist and is telling us his story, it is because the first person functions here somewhat as it does in Henry James' *The Aspern Papers*: the narrator, in putting down his confession and in believing that he is in control, is confessing a reality different from his own. But there will always be an ambiguity, a deliberate question at the heart of the novel: for, if Hermann, a bit of a fool as well as a madman, confesses early that he is a liar, we should remember that all artists are, in a sense, liars.

Nabokov, the artist, the original creator, accepts the existence of his character, his "I," even to the point of making moral judgments about him. In his foreword to *Despair*, he compares Hermann Karlovich and Humbert Humbert, the narrator of "a much later novel." But "Hermann and Humbert are alike only in the sense that two dragons painted by the same artist at different periods of his life resemble each other. Both are neurotic scoundrels, yet there is a green lane in Paradise where Humbert is permitted to wander at

dusk once a year; but Hell shall never parole Hermann" (9). Here the differences are more important than the similarities. Hermann Karlovich, though, is not just a neurotic scoundrel; he is quite insane. The use of the madman as "hero" is an old one in both English and Russian literature: the father of Nabokov's madman (indeed, of all his madmen) is Nikolai Gogol. Hermann, for instance, refers to Gogol's *Memoirs of a Madman*, although he does not quite remember the title — a failure on Hermann's part to be both an exact scholar and an artist capable of discovering exact relationships. Hermann's failure is Nabokov's way of suggesting to us that the madman is never important to the artist as just a case study; the madman as "hero" calls our attention to questions of reality, to questions of what we are ourselves.

To disturb our sense of the real by disturbing our expectations, Nabokov puts himself momentarily into the novel: Hermann intends his first reader to be a certain émigré "Russian author. . . . the well-known author of psychological novels." This reader he addresses directly: "What will you feel, reader-writer, when you tackle my tale? Delight? Envy? Or even . . . who knows? . . . you may use my termless removal to give out my stuff for your own . . . for the fruit of your own crafty . . . and experienced imagination; leaving me out in the cold" (90 - 91). This well-known Russian author, of non-psychological novels which "cannot possibly appear in the U.S.S.R." (168), has done so.

We do not know, however, at the beginning that Hermann is mad and that Nabokov is writing the novel. These facts are revealed by the usual indirection. For example, in describing his wife and their lovemaking, Hermann suddenly tells of having perceived that "the violence and the sweetness of my nightly joys were being raised to an exquisite vertex owing to a certain aberration which, I understand, is not as uncommon as I thought at first among high-strung men in their middle thirties. I am referring to a well-known kind of 'dissociation' " (37). He then relates how he has found himself dividing into two: he is both making love to his wife and observing himself doing so. And, as time goes on, he finds it is incumbent for him to move farther and farther from his double in the bed, always watching, always separate. "Eventually I found myself sitting in the parlor — while making love in the bedroom. It was not enough" (38). But much of this, maybe all of it, has been taking place in his mind since one night, when he has just split himself, he hears his wife calling to him; he is actually sitting in the parlor; he has not

even gone to bed. And so the spell is broken — for him. For he has subtly led us to accept his split as actual, and it takes time for us to stand back, and look.

But this theme of the creative, tricking artist and of the madman is directly brought together in this early assertion of Hermann's:

I have grown much too used to an outside view of myself, to being both painter and model, so no wonder my style is denied the blessed grace of spontaneity. Try as I may I do not succeed in getting back into my original envelope, let alone making myself comfortable in my old self; the disorder there is far too great; things have been moved, the lamp is black and dead, bits of my past litter the floor (29).

Here we are given not only the artist and the madman but Nabokov himself; for Nabokov makes sure that his madman believes in "the blessed grace of spontaneity," a yielding of artistic control to a haphazard and unartistic "inspiration," one more "idea" that Nabokov finds antipathetic.

We are also told, by another indirection, how and why Hermann is writing his confessions. For, although we are not told clearly until very late in the narrative, he is composing his book while he is hiding in the Pyrenees. There is too, in both Russian and English, an occasional revelatory time shift. If most of the book is given in conventional past tenses, we suddenly find sentences that are in the present: "I think I ought to inform the reader that there has just been a long interval. The sun has had time to set, touching up on its way down with sanguine the clouds above the Pyrenean mountain that so resembles Fujiyama" (15). ("Pyrenean" is not in the original Russian; here the Russian is more reticent than the English. It does not do to speed-read Nabokov.)

And so there is a further irony in that, as Claire Rosenfield points out, Hermann's "crime is part of his deep-buried longing to be an artist. . . . The nature of a crime is like that of 'every art.' "[7] The crime will be, however, an act in the world; and it cannot be revised. The artist gets but one chance; here he is truly spontaneous, even if he has planned ahead. And in Hermann's failure to achieve true spontaneity the crime fails, for he cannot respond to the unexpected.

There is more mockery, this time Hermann's, but also Nabokov's of Hermann, in Hermann's musing about Felix, death, and art: "We had identical features, and . . . in a state of perfect repose, this resemblance was strikingly evident, and what is death, if not a face

at peace — its artistic perfection? Life only marred my double; thus
a breeze dims the bliss of Narcissus . . ." (25). Art is not life, in the
simple sense that says that it should be only feeling, or action, or
reflection; but art is life in that it is, as well as represents, movement.
The failed artist, like Hermann, thinks of art as mere stasis, as death.
Hermann cannot, then, recognize art, any more than he can recognize people — and the failures are one and the same. Ardalion
makes a pastel portrait of Hermann, and, in Hermann's words, the
invited viewers

stood and gaped; at what? At the ruddy horror of my face. I do not know
why he had lent my cheeks that fruity hue; they are really as pale as death.
Look as one might, none could see the ghost of a likeness! How utterly
ridiculous, for instance, that crimson point in the canthus, or that glimpse of
eyetooth from under a curled, snarly lip. All this — against an ambitious
background hinting at things that might have been either geometrical
figures or gallow trees. . . . (66)

Ardalion's portrait is obviously more insightful than Hermann can
bear — and most prophetic.

On the day the portrait is finished, Hermann begins to act. He
writes a letter to Felix, saying that "I have found some work for you.
First of all we must have an eye-to-eye monologue and get things
settled." And later he adds, "I cannot recollect now if the
'monologue' was a slip or a joke" (69). It is Hermann's slip,
Nabokov's joke. Felix is late to their meeting, and Hermann says, "I
somehow found myself thinking that Felix could not come for the
simple reason that he was a product of my imagination, which
hankered after reflections, repetitions, masks . . ." (80). The double,
Hermann-Nabokov, is speaking now as the artist-creator; for Felix is,
in a sense, Hermann's creation, just as Hermann is Nabokov's. And
art is a many faceted-bewildering mirror; as Hermann observes,
"The invention of art contain[s] far more intrinsical truth than life's
reality" (132).

Hermann pretends to be an actor seeking an understudy; but this
pretense — this role-playing, and this attempt at one kind of identity
— makes Felix suspicious. At last Hermann hints that there is to be a
crime; Felix, in Hermann's clothes, will supply the alibi. Crime is
the magic word for Felix, as it is for Hermann who now tells Lydia
that he has found a long-lost brother who has, after a life of crime,
decided to commit suicide, but who wishes to do his brother Hermann a good turn by pretending to be Hermann and by going into

the grave as Hermann. Lydia, after a certain protest, consents. And so the crime is carried out. The last two chapters (ten and eleven) of the novel are devoted to Hermann's musings about his crime and to his actions after the murder — to the search for meaning. He speaks to his reader, telling him that he "longed, to the point of pain, for that masterpiece of mine (finished and signed on the ninth of March in a gloomy wood) to be appreciated by men, or in other words, for the deception — and every work of art is a deception — to act successfully; as to the royalties, so to speak, paid by the insurance firm, that was in my mind a matter of secondary importance. Oh, yes, I was the pure artist of romance" (188). Nabokov himself says, "Art is a magical deception, as all nature is magic and deception."[8]

Hermann now imagines that Lydia will rejoin him and that all will be well. But she does not come, and he finally learns from the newspapers that his perfect crime was just a crime and that "the murderer's identity was known, and . . . that of the victim was not" (195). His work of art has deceived no one because it was not a work of art — although, characteristically, he accuses the police of incredible stupidity. For they do not seem to understand what he has done at all; they cannot perceive that Felix is Hermann's double. Hermann is almost content, though, since, as we have noted, he is living under Felix's name, which he believes is untraceable. However, names are once again deceiving, even if Hermann announces, "I look like my name, gentlemen, and it fits me as exactly as it used to fit him. You must be fools not to understand" (203). But, still reading the papers, he finds that the German police have discovered "the murdered man's identity," which he first misreads as "the murderer's identity" (209), something they already knew.

"Reality," then, has its revenge even upon Hermann's written work; he had originally planned only ten chapters, but he now must write another to describe his feelings and his flight. His "tale degenerates into a diary," like Gogol's *Memoirs of a Madman*; and a diary "is the lowest form of literature" (218). This diary covers only two days, March 31 and April 1, that date so significant to Nabokov. The March 31 entry ends with "What on earth have I done?" (220). April 1, the day of fools, opens with the police at the gate. And Hermann asks himself and writes down: "How about opening the window and making a little speech[?]" (221) to the crowd gathered in the street below: "Frenchmen! This is a rehearsal. Hold those policemen. A famous film actor will presently come running out of this house. He is an arch-criminal but he must escape" (222). To the end,

Hermann is planning a role, trying to be the artist creating himself, the movie actor at last who acts in the actual world.

And, of course, because he is a failed artist, we are left unsure as to whether he exists or not, at the same moment that he has existed, since Nabokov created him. But art, once more, has told us that we cannot be sure of reality; only art, giving us insight into irrationality, may be trusted.

III   Invitation to a Beheading (Priglashenie na kazn')

In 1938, Nabokov published his drama, *The Waltz Invention*, a dream play in which a madman envisages himself, through the power of a wonder weapon, as absolute world dictator. The madman's intentions are admirable; but, since his character is human, all his noble intentions are lost in the intoxication of power. In the end, reality reenters; and the spectators perceive that the central character is insane. But madness and politics are closely allied.

In that same year, Nabokov published the dream novel *Priglashenie na kazn'* (*Invitation to a Beheading*). Politics and the reality of politics are also this novel's subjects, but they are much less obvious. For *Invitation* is one of his most difficult, evasive works; and it is unlike any other. Its difficulty is not in its language, neither in English nor in the original Russian, but in its setting, form, and characters; for nowhere else are Nabokov's story line, the place, and the people so indefinite. In some unnamed dream country, the young man, Cincinnatus C., is condemned to death by beheading for "gnostical turpitude," a crime that does not exist for us in law or perhaps even in conception. Cincinnatus spends his last days in an absurd jail where he is visited by shape-changing jailers, an executioner who pretends to be a prisoner, and by his wife's family, who not only crowd the jail cell with themselves but bring along furniture. When, at the last, Cincinnatus is led out to be executed, by an act of will he denies the existence of his executioners; and they vanish quite away along with the whole world they inhabit. Nowhere else does Nabokov present a social scene so thin, one that makes the almost diaphanous otherworldly existence of the Russian émigrés of *Mashenka* appear sturdy and enduring; and, compared to the setting of *Invitation*, the invented countries and planets of *Pale Fire* and *Ada* are thoroughly realistic. Nowhere else, too, can Nabokov so easily be accused of deliberately creating unreal, unbelievable caricatures of people for no identifiable purpose. The novel has no time or place and the reader is left on the edge of the unknown. And Nabokov is unwilling to give its "ideas," always insisting upon the lack of value of ideas in art.

This "vagueness" is carried even into the book's title — but it also suggests that this vagueness is only apparent, not real. *Priglashenie na kazn'* means, more literally but less euphonically than the final English title, "Invitation to an Execution." As Nabokov points out in his foreword to the English version, he has done relatively little "rewriting" of this novel in its translation. "My Russian idiom, in 1935, had embodied a certain vision in the precise terms that fitted it. . . . and [since] fidelity to one's author comes first," the book was "literally" translated.[9] And so these titles and their meanings, this story, if obscure, are so because they are presenting an obscurity precisely. And yet what do we do with a casual social invitation to a terrible ritual which ends in death?

We should note that the book was written in Berlin "in one fortnight of wonderful excitement and sustained inspiration"[10] "some fifteen years after [Nabokov's] escaping from the Bolshevist regime, and just before the Nazi regime reached its full volume of welcome" (5). And we should also note both that Cincinnatus is sentenced to death for a crime against the community, the collectivity, the state; and that this crime, "gnostical turpitude, [is] so rare and so unutterable that it was necessary to use circumlocutions like 'impenetrability,' 'opacity,' 'occlusion' . . ." (72). Or, as expressed elsewhere, "he was impervious to the rays of others" (24), these others who can see into and be seen into without difficulty; the true members of the collectivity understand "each other at the first word, since they had no words that would end in an unexpected way . . ." (26). The novel seems, then, if we are to take the situation presented and the time of its composition into consideration, to be primarily about politics, an unusual (surface) concern either for the young Nabokov — despite *The Waltz Invention* — or for the old Nabokov. However, Cincinnatus' "crime" and this language about language are the clues to the book's meanings, but those meanings are not to be given simply.

Moreover, the form of the book is odd, a literary experiment that we would not expect Nabokov to make; for it is, at first glance, an allegory or, more precisely, it approaches the allegorical. Of all fictional forms, the one Nabokov probably has the least affection for is the allegory since it, with its messages, is in the end only message.

Certainly, though, any work which deliberately chooses flat characters runs the risk of being considered allegorical — and Nabokov's
characters are flat.

Yet the action of the novel is something else, even if it does take
place in that undefined world; it is not a neat laying down of events
which take their meanings from some other level of human life. Cincinnatus' adventures are self-contained, although they are, no doubt,
comments about the world of politics, of morality, of psychology.
They are, as Khodasevich argued, comments about and
demonstrations of art, of creativity; and, therefore, they are comments about and demonstrations of man's existence. This "existentialist" term is not to be taken to mean that Nabokov is sympathetic
with existentialism or existentialists — he regards Sartre as a rather
simpleminded moralist. But Nabokov cannot avoid talking about
man and man's place in the universe.

As epigraph, Nabokov appends a quotation from his "favorite
author," "the melancholy, extravagant, wise, witty, magical, and
altogether delightful Pierre Delalande, whom I invented" (6) and
who is, therefore, Nabokov himself. In *Discours sur les ombres* (the
words "ombres," "shadow," "almost *hombre*," haunt Nabokov's
English works), Delalande declares: "Comme un fou se croit Dieu,
nous nous croyons mortels" (10): "As a madman believes himself
God, we believe ourselves mortal." An insanely true paradox exists
here: a madman is a kind of artist who is a creator — and so we may
be immortal, at least in art.

The immortality of art is, to repeat, a victory over time, although
time always remains the essence of mystery. Cincinnatus wishes to
be out of the time in which he exists: "there is a rare kind of time in
which I live — the pause, the hiatus, when the heart is like a feather
. . ." (53). His true life is elsewhere, then, beyond his stifling community — an elsewhere in which history, with its horrors, can be escaped. And Nabokov gives Cincinnatus the image of the rug as time
that is almost the same as the one he gives himself in *Speak,
Memory.*[11] Cincinnatus thinks of that other world: "*there* the freaks
that are tortured here walked unmolested; *there* time takes shape according to one's pleasure, like a figured rug whose folds can be
gathered in such a way that two designs will meet — and the rug is
once again smoothed out, and you live on, or else superimpose the
next image on the last, endlessly, endlessly . . ." (94). This world is,
as I have suggested, and with all cautions appended, a Platonic one
— Nabokov's world of personal time which is a permanent present.

But *Invitation* is not always quite this serious; it is also a Nabokovian comedy in which the humor is set against the sinister threat contained in the title. Commenting on it, mocking it, the humor makes it human. It is a humor of language, that highest of human acts — and it is in the language, the *how* of the novel, that we can also best see the way Nabokov not only can do almost the same comic, meaningful thing but tries to do it, line for line, in the Russian and English version. At one moment, when Cincinnatus is being visited by his wife's family, a brother-in-law tells him in the English version, "Take the word 'anxiety'. . . . Now take away the word 'tiny'." (103). "Anxiety," minus a "tiny" bit, becomes, of course, "axe." In the Russian version, the brother-in-law asks Cincinnatus to consider the word "ropot," or "murmur." Then, he goes on, "Now spell it backwards." And "topor" means "axe." The English is probably more functional, more comic, than the Russian in this case; but the pattern holds true for the whole novel.

Other examples of comedy are the same in both languages; the translation carries them over. For instance, we have the comedy of event: "Sometime later Rodion the jailer came in and offered to dance a waltz with him. Cincinnatus agreed." Or we find the comedy of cartoon caricature: the prison director, Rodrig, wears "a perfect toupee, black as pitch, and with a waxy parting. . . . His face, selected without love . . . was enlivened in a sense by two, and only by two, bulging eyes" (13 - 14, 15). This humor, this destruction of officialdom and state power through language, is the means by which Nabokov brings together the theme of art with the theme of politics. Robert Alter suggests the solution:[12] Cincinnatus is, as artist, insisting upon creating his own world against the pressures of "reality," which is, in this case, a mask for "society." But the society is totalitarian   Nabokov could not avoid his own time and place; and the Bolshevist and Nazi totalitarianisms are the present manifestations of the threat that exists behind the novel.

The novel opens with the pronouncement of the death sentence which is uttered "in a whisper" "in accordance with the law," and already societal law is made absurd. Cincinnatus, a rather meek, small man, is taken "back to the fortress," there to be left in solitude by the jailer, his lawyer, and even the authorial voice, who now addresses the reader directly in a weird apostrophe:

So we are nearing the end. The right-hand, still untasted part of the novel, which, during our delectable reading, we would lightly feel, mechanically testing whether there were still plenty left (and our fingers were always gladdened by the placid, faithful thickness) has suddenly, for no reason at all, become quite meager: a few minutes of quick reading, already downhill, and — O horrible! (12)

And, although most of the book remains to be read, we *are* nearing the end. With Cincinnatus' condemnation, the reader, who is also a creator who is living in this world of the artist, is also aware of time, of ending.

But, for the moment, both Cincinnatus and the reader are in this comic, nightmare world. Cincinnatus is visited by the prison director, who responds to Cincinnatus' questions about when the death sentence will be carried out by "unfortunately I myself do not know. I am always informed at the last moment." Then he adds, with that incongruous, irrational logic of the book but also of the archetypal bureaucrat, "I have complained many times and can show you all the correspondence on the subject if you are interested" (15 - 16). The logic of the jail is, then, the logic of irrationality, a mockery and a satire of rationality — and the society around Cincinnatus acts with precisely the illogic of mystery that is found in the world depicted by Kafka. Nabokov, in the foreword, denies that he was influenced by Kafka but adds that, "if I did have to choose a kindred soul, it would certainly be that great artist rather than G. H. Orwell or other popular purveyors of illustrated ideas and publicistic fiction" (6). In an interview he indicated that "there are affinities between *Invitation to a Beheading* and *The Castle*, but I had not yet read Kafka when I wrote my novel."[13] Kafka's books reveal the mystery; Orwell's are only images of the time.

Cincinnatus does know the crime for which he has been convicted; he is not the existentialist hero or victim in any real sense, for it is not a matter of everyone being lost in a purposeless world. Cincinnatus has been found to be different, not a member; and therefore by law he must die — and all the forms of law are followed exactly in the trial and in its aftermath. The basic situation in the novel may be absurd, illogical; but its working out is not; this "actuality" is, perversely, the world of the paranoid.

Cincinnatus' opacity is actual and, at the same time, a sign of other incongruities, individualities. For example, in conversation with his lawyer, he becomes irritated at the lawyer's sudden refusal, inability, to answer why there is no commonsense in the whole set of institutions or people controlling Cincinnatus' case. The lawyer now

cries, "It is exactly for that tone . . . ," and Cincinnatus finishes the
sentence with "that I am being executed" (37). The punishment for
this refusal to fit in is, of course, appropriate. The opaque Cincinnatus must be made transparent, unindividual, even before that final
transparency — since we are all alike then — of death. In the cell,
Cincinnatus has no privacy. People continually intrude. Worse, the
peephole is so set as to allow him no place to hide. Therefore, "Cincinnatus did not crumple the motley newspapers, did not hurl them,
as his double did (the double, the gangrel, that accompanies each of
us — you, and me, and him over there — doing what we would like
to do at that very moment, but cannot . . .)" (25). This "me" is once
more the authorial voice defining our terms for us — being moral
despite these disclaimers. For the double here is our dream self, that
aspect of ourselves which fulfills our wishes; and wishes are the rejections of the standards of society. If the standards of society are immoral, the rejections are moral: here, then, the double is Cincinnatus' opaqueness, the refusal to be a carbon copy.

To be like everyone else is, of course, to be utterly visible, to be
named. Momentarily, Nabokov reveals his distrust of, not his faith
in, language. For the normal people of the novel everything exists
because it is named: "*That which does not have a name does not exist.* Unfortunately everything had a name" (26). The artist,
Nabokov-Cincinnatus, adds this "unfortunately"; for denying existence to the unnamed is a denial of mystery and of the possibility of
human choice. Oddly enough, Cincinnatus has not chosen to be
different; he was simply born that way — perhaps *poeta nascitur,
non fit* (a poet is born, not made). And with one more of Nabokov's
deliberate doublings of time that show not only how all things are
related — the present and the past occur in the same paragraph —
but also how one may be chosen out by the mystery, we are given
Cincinnatus' life story — his illegitimate birth, his almost unconscious childish awareness of his difference, and his attempts at
concealment. We are given, in brief, not only his difference but his
loneliness — and these make him more human than all the rest.

"At fifteen Cincinnatus went to work in the toy workshop," making rag dolls: "little hairy Pushkin in a fur carrick, and ratlike Gogol
in a flamboyant waistcoat, and old little Tolstoy with his fat
nose . . . ," all these actual Russian writers of the novel's "mythical
Nineteenth Century . . ." (27). For these men, with their insights
into the human, have become reduced to dolls in a mythical century;
the most real of things are denied. It is fitting, therefore, that Cincin-

natus should meet in the toy workshop the girl, Marthe, who will become his wife — and be continually unfaithful to him. He courts her in the Tamara Gardens (an odd prefigurement or echo, of Nabokov's own life, since these gardens have the same name as the Tamara of *Speak, Memory* — a name which was not her real one and which Nabokov borrows from *Invitation*). These gardens are a Garden of Eden that is too perfect, too mechanical, to be paradise. The gardens are, in short, the natural world as perceived by an unnatural society, one without true feeling.

Marthe bears two children, neither of them Cincinnatus'. "The boy was lame and evil-tempered, the girl dull, obese and nearly blind" (31). This use of the cripple as a symbol of evil is not an insensitive act on Nabokov's part. This act is, first, the standard literary device; and, second, the children are not brought alive for the reader — they are simply signals of the evil of the society in which they exist. But, more, they are signs of each other, doubles and opposites, always a threat. Paradoxically, but expectedly, Cincinnatus stops watching himself after their births; he stops hiding his opacity by trickery; one day he is seen as he really is; and a few days later he is arrested, tried, and sentenced. But the two children are repeated: both outside and inside the prison, the actuality of evil is multiplied: now doubleness is sameness, unindividuality, evil. Cincinnatus imagines Marthe as being followed by "a dark-mustachioed young blade" and then "by a fair-haired fop . . ." (73 - 74); and, when she and her family come to visit him, her brothers arrive too, "identical twins except that one had a golden mustache and the other a pitch-black one" (98). The hint of incest is in the duplicity.

Inside the prison, on the other hand, Cincinnatus is the *only* prisoner. But he is continually visited by his lawyer, Roman Vissarionovich (this name echoes Stalin's and contains its own threat); by the prison director, Rodrig; and by the jailer, Rodion. These three "R's" tend to blend into one another; in fact, they are at times one another. In short, Cincinnatus cannot escape the cruelty of likenesses. These three visitors are complemented by the brilliantly presented M'sieur Pierre, the fat, athletic, egotistical little man who is to be Cincinnatus' executioner; for, although Pierre is "different," he is false. He does not look at all like Cincinnatus; he does not act like him; he is, rather, voluble, energetic, and insensitive. Yet he comes to live in the prison as a pretended prisoner in order to reduce Cincinnatus to the level of them all — by so forcing himself upon

Cincinnatus that they will be one, doubles: Cincinnatus will be made transparent.

But Pierre's mission fails. Although Pierre plays tricks on Cincinnatus and although he betrays him, he cannot break Cincinnatus' will; nor can he understand, himself, this otherness. At every moment Pierre is defeated, even though he rebounds with all the energy of evil. But only on the last night, when they go in obedience to the inflexible mad law to a party does Pierre suffer his final defeat. He asks Cincinnatus to drink with him, then demands it, and is at the last reduced to pouring wine over both their heads. Symbolically, when the landscape is illumined by a "grandiose monogram of 'P' and 'C' " in light bulbs, it does "not quite come off" (189). And, fittingly, on the next day, as the stage setting of the whole city collapses, Pierre is carried off by a woman who holds him "like a larva in her arms" (223). The original Latin meaning for "larva" is "ghost," although by metonymy it also signified a "mask."

Besides Cincinnatus, the other seeming individual in this world of repetitions and falsities is little Emmie, the prison director's daughter. Of this strange, fey child Nabokov remarks in his introduction that "the evil-minded will perceive in [her] . . . a sister of little Lolita" (7 - 8). Cincinnatus wants to believe that Emmie shares something with him, a sharing that is human, not mechanical. When she sneaks into his cell, he muses, "If only you were grown up, . . . if your soul had a slight touch of my patina, you would, as in poetic antiquity, feed a potion to the turnkey, on a night that is murky" (47). But she too betrays him; for she, like M'sieur Pierre, is not what she seems. After casually leading him unknowingly back into the prison — indeed into her father's apartment where everyone else is gathered on the day he thinks he is escaping, she "sat down at the table . . . and having dismissed Cincinnatus forever, began spreading sugar" on a piece of melon. And it is now that Pierre makes a pass at her which everyone else ignores since Pierre is important — and she is, despite appearances, his instrument (166 - 67).

It is almost necessary then that it be little Emmie who figures in the demonstration that Pierre, who fancies himself an artist, is a false artist; he is only an imitator. Pierre makes a "photohoroscope" of her, a series of photographs in which her head is attached to various bodies — and in which she is shown growing up, growing old — but they are palpable fakes intended as truth. Therefore, they lack both the validity of parody and the strength of holding time at bay. But, of course, in a false world all pictures are false. The reality, the present world of Cincinnatus, is also a stage setting, a parody. At one moment, Cincinnatus, let out of his cell, discovers Emmie in a corridor; she walks to a niche where there is a window; but the window is "only the semblance of a window; actually it was a glazed recess, a showcase," and it displays "a view of the Tamara Gardens," a badly executed view (76), just as we would expect. The fake is parodied.

We are given hints of that other, better, more real world which are presented, not so oddly, in terms of the past. Cincinnatus, in leafing through a magazine, "published once upon a time, in a barely remembered age," is able to find pictures of a former reality. This "once upon a time" suggests a fairy tale, but the point is much more solid; for those pictures are varied, complex, not reduced to a oneness. The objects they offer "sparkled with youth and an inborn insolence, proceeding from the reverence that surrounded the labor devoted to their manufacture" (50). In this world, the worker is not alienated from his product; it is the world of nuances, of differences — the world of the artist and, so, of humanity.

But the novel's themes are given directly in Cincinnatus' words as the book draws toward its actual end and toward Cincinnatus' execution:

> Everything has fallen into place, that is, everything has duped me — all of this theatrical, pathetic stuff — the promises of a volatile maiden, a mother's moist gaze, the knocking on the wall, a neighbor's friendliness, and, finally, those hills which broke out in a deadly rash. . . . This is the dead end of this life, and I should not have sought salvation within its confines. . . . I have discovered the little crack in life . . . where it had once been soldered to something else, something genuinely alive, important and vast. . . . (204 - 5).

Immediately after Cincinnatus records these words, Pierre arrives with Roman Vissarionovich and Rodrig to take Cincinnatus to his death. Cincinnatus, given a list of last wishes and told to choose one, demands his own thing, "To finish writing something," but then he "suddenly understood that everything had in fact been written already" (209). The sense is contained in an earlier exchange: after Pierre has pretended to have been arrested for plotting Cincinnatus' escape, Cincinnatus says that he has "surmised" that someone else might be trying to rescue him. When Pierre asks him who this "savior" is, Cincinnatus replies simply, "Imagination" (114).

The novel has been written, its world built; now it is time to transcend that novel and that world by showing that they transcend themselves; the artist's act is both internal and external to ourselves. And so Cincinnatus leaves on his final ride through the streets in order to complete the one artistic act and to go on to the next. If it is a world of others, of political acts, of social acts, of acts which demand absolute conformity, likeness, and so death, which the artist must face, it is, at the last, his right and his ability to leap the bounds of that world by the creative act. This creative act enables Cincinnatus to ask himself, as he is lying on the block, "Why am I here? Why am I lying like this? And, having asked himself these simple questions, he answered them by getting up and looking around" (222). And the world of appearances collapses.

The ending of the novel may seem ambiguous — there are two Cincinnatuses, the one who counts to ten as a signal to Pierre, the executioner, and the one who stands up. But the ambiguity suggests that reality must impinge upon us — that we cannot escape it corporally at the same moment that we may do so imaginatively. The final images of the novel are not of just escape but of overcoming falsity; for "amidst the dust, and the falling things, and the flapping scenery, Cincinnatus made his way in that direction where, to judge by the voices, stood beings akin to him" (223). One Cincinnatus may have died — the political, social Cincinnatus; but the creative Cincinnatus has lived, overcoming through imagination the unreality of time.

CHAPTER 5

The Russian Masterpiece

IT is almost universally agreed among those who have read
Nabokov's works in Russian that *Dar* (*The Gift*) is his finest novel
in his mother language. Andrew Field, in fact, claims that "it is the
greatest novel Russian literature has yet produced in this century."[1]
Nabokov himself feels that *Dar* is "the best" of his Russian novels.[2]
But it is also one of Nabokov's most Russian works; for, as he says in
the foreword to the English translation (1963), "Its heroine is not
Zina, but Russian Literature" —[3] and he is nearly correct. The novel
is about Russian literature; but it is also about love, and, by indirection, politics. It is, in brief, about man.

Concretely, the novel is about the life and artistic development of
Fyodor Godunov — Cherdyntsev, a young Russian exile in Berlin.
His life, outside his work, is in his almost meeting, then meeting,
falling in love with, and wooing the girl, Zina Mertz, as well as in his
contacts with other Russian émigrés. But the novel, divided into five
chapters, each of which has a language-literature theme, is also
about three dead people about whose lives Fyodor is asked to write
and of one of whose he does: the young boy, Yasha Chernyshevski,
who committed suicide; Fyodor's father, who disappeared in Asia;
and the historically actual Nikolay Gavrilovich Chernyshevski, the
one "life" Fyodor succeeds in recording.

What the novel does is to bring together Nabokov's worlds of the
time. But, ironically, perhaps bitterly, Nabokov says it is "the last
novel I wrote, or ever shall write, in Russian." Published serially in
Sovremennye Zapiski in 1937 - 1938 without the controversial,
"political," fourth chapter (the life of Chernyshevski), the novel was
not printed as a complete book until 1952. The English translation
may have been, as Nabokov asserts, "especially hard" because of
"the participation of so many Russian muses within the orchestration

of the novel" (10); but it has become a remarkable English novel too. Certain Russian allusions disappear; certain Russian sound patterns which connect worlds are lost; but the English version finds, if not equivalents, analogues — as in the lovely play on the name of the heroine, Zina: "What shall I call you? Half-Mnemo*syne* [that is, Zina, coupled with the Greek word for Memory]? There's a half-shim*mer* in your surname too" (169). And the English "shimmer" both translates Zina's name and contains it — the Russian for "shimmer" is "*merts*anie."

Apart from *Speak, Memory*, this novel is Nabokov's most personal work. This time, though, he is not using his childhood and adolescence but the world of Berlin — one much more realized than in *Mashenka*. In this novel he is not trying to write about himself, except, as I have suggested, as any artist uses his work as a means of self-knowledge; instead this work is a portrait of the artist in the process of becoming an artist, and his own most intimate knowledge of the process is Nabokov's subject. The novel is, for that matter, his first and only novel in which the major figure — if we do not count Sebastian Knight or John Shade, for each of them is subordinate to the narrator of their respective works — is an actual creative artist, not a failure. In this case, the protagonist, Fyodor, is a novelist-poet whose first important work, the one that he finally achieves within the narrative of this novel, is paradoxically a biography, no novel and no *biographie romancée*, of an actual historical figure.

And so the novel *is* about literature by the back door; but, as we noted before, it is not only about Russian literature. For it develops the Nabokovian thesis that no one is a writer who has not made the literature of his language, as well as his language and his life, completely his own, so that he may reshape it, reuse it, until it is new art — not fact, not biography, not confession or simple expression — that presents insight into the mystery of the world. If *The Gift* seems to echo Joyce's *Portrait of the Artist as a Young Man*, it is really more about art than Joyce's novel is and less about the suffering artist's rebellion, alienation, and exile. Nabokov's work, longer, and more diffuse, is also less deadly serious than Joyce's at the same time that it actually involves more "life" with its art.

But, since Nabokov's novel is also about politics, it is about the growth of the artist's awareness of values. Fyodor, writing about Chernyshevski, the antipathetic social critic of the nineteenth century, begins "to comprehend by degrees that such uncompromising radicals as Chernyshevski, with all their ludicrous and ghastly blunders, were, no matter how you looked at it, real heroes in their struggle with the governmental order of things" (214 - 15).

Nevertheless, the novel, in itself, is once more the main concern. "It is a novel of tenuously connected short stories," Field asserts, adding that it "is plotted according to intricate analogy and coincidence."[4] Both statements are accurate, for it is a bewilderingly complex work. Its five chapters cover Russian émigré life in Berlin during the middle 1920s, with flashbacks, excursions, and a brilliant evocation of life in the nineteenth century in the Chernyshevski biography. We might take, as a clue, the epigraph which, like most such things in Nabokov, is both a joke and a serious assertion:

An oak is a tree. A rose is a flower. A deer is an animal. A sparrow is a bird. Russia is our fatherland. Death is inevitable.
— P. Smirnovski, *A Textbook of Russian Grammar*

This epigraph, Nabokov says, "is not a fabrication" (11). It is, rather, a real introduction to the novel that gives us its shape as well as a hint of its subject matter; for these apparently disparate and naive assertions contain the natural world; Russia, things Russian, and the Russian language; and our inevitable fate, which art, this novel, transcends, denies, overcomes, and teaches us to accept. The novel contains, in short, all those subject matters of Nabokov as artist; but it does so by indirect and parodic analogy and by coincidence.

Even the first line of the novel itself does not let the attentive and creative reader be misled: the date is given as "April the first, 192 -," and immediately the parodic tone is established. Moreover, the movingvan parked on a Berlin street that the author now describes has no real function in the novel although it is portentously introduced: it upsets our expectations since it introduces us at best to some minor characters who occasionally step onto the novel's stage and whose real importance is that they know Zina Mertz, the "heroine," the girl whom Fyodor meets much later and with whom he falls in love. Yet the van, the two people waiting on the sidewalk for their furniture, and the April day have an artistic function. They are observed by an "I" who sees them while standing "on the sidewalk, before the house (in which I too shall dwell)" (15); and this "I" becomes on the next page the "he" who is Fyodor. Such a beginning is one more manipulation of reality. And all this imagery is revealed as half-fantasy, all art, when Fyodor thinks, "Some day . . . I must use such a scene to start a good, thick old-fashioned novel"

(16). What follows, of course, is that novel; but it is hardly old-fashioned. At the end of the book, Fyodor, talking to Zina, is planning the novel he has all along been preparing himself for — a novel that is, of course, this one; this gift, the gift. He has been writing it while living it.

But, Fyodor says to Zina at the end, "the most enchanting things in nature and art are based on deception. [Our story] began with a reckless impetuosity and ended with the finest of finishing touches. Now isn't that the plot for a remarkable novel? What a theme! But it must be built up, curtained, surrounded by dense life — my life, my professional passions and cares." When she responds, "Yes, but that will result in an autobiography with mass executions of good acquaintances," he replies that he will so reshape it that what will remain of the autobiography will be only dust, "the kind of dust . . . which makes the most orange of skies."

She tells him he will be "such a writer as has never been before," which is an ambiguous phrase; and then she demands, in a startling and seemingly irrelevant non sequitur, "But do you love me?" He answers, "What I am saying is in fact a kind of declaration of love" (376). And that is what he has been asserting in all the work; love for the woman, the human being, is love for the art, love for the complex thing he has just lived and will write — has written.

Once more the novel is structurally a working out of its own themes: it is built in its own spiral, the beginning is contained in the end but has become different; it is the author's personal wrestling with time, a victory and a defeat. The work both exists in and tells a story in linear time but also comments upon itself from an eternal present outside the lineal progression. Nevertheless, we must grant that the novel is a congeries of stories that are held together only by the personality and experiences of Fyodor — we must grant this only, of course, only to deny it. Even Fyodor's story is not single; he takes half the book to meet Zina, half a book before the human love story can begin; he has friends, actual conversations, imaginary conversations, enemies, and half of them never impinge upon the other half.

Then, there is the "biography" of the dead Yasha Chernyshevski who wrote poetry and committed suicide for love, a biography which Fyodor, who did not know Yasha, is asked to write but which he does not want to write and does not write — but which is told to us anyway, by Nabokov — who is, here, Fyodor, the artist feeling his way through a story he cannot put on paper — yet. There is also the biography of Fyodor's father, which his mother asks him to write, a biography which he wants to compose as a matter of filial piety; which he plans out, does the research for, and cannot, finally, compose — and which is also told to us, through fact and dreamlike sequences.

There is, finally, the life and death, the biography, of Nikolay Gavrilovich Chernyshevski. This real nineteenth-century Russian radical is the antithesis, as I have suggested, in esthetic ideals, political beliefs, and some personal ideas, to Fyodor — and Nabokov — whose life, nevertheless, Fyodor — and thus Nabokov — does write, at great length. The editors of *Sovremennye Zapiski* would not publish this chapter in the original printing of the novel, "for," Nabokov reports, "the same reasons that the biography it contains was rejected" by Nabokov's own character, Georgiy Ivanovich Vasiliev, who edits the *Gazeta*, the liberal émigré journal, in this very novel. As Nabokov states, we have here "a pretty example of life finding itself obliged to imitate the very art it condemns" (9). The insight into the relationship of life and art that is given is more than the expression of an artist who finds his position justified.

But we must remember that all of these stories are the products of Fyodor's mind. In short, these stories are truly all one since they are aspects of, parts of, the central figure, the artist creating himself, although we must make a qualification, for it is not simply a matter of creating oneself — the artist is the man with genius who then acts in the world. But this artistic creation is both conscious and unconscious. If, at the beginning, Fyodor thinks of writing this "thick old-fashioned novel," this "fleeting thought was touched with a careless irony; an irony, however, that was quite unnecessary, because somebody within him, on his behalf, independently from him, had absorbed all this, recorded it, and filed it away" (16). This "somebody," the artistic memory, will give it back to him when he needs it.

Fyodor has just published his first book of poems in this beginning: and Nabokov says that "the plot of Chapter One centers in Fyodor's poems" (10). But these are both true poems and parodied poems: Nabokov recites a later poem, "The Swift," in his Spoken Arts recording of readings from his works, and notes Fyodor as "original author," thereby creating one of those odd, echoing, parodically serious relationships in which an author gives his poem to a character who is not quite himself and makes the poem a double, ambivalent thing.

But the "discussion" of the poems in *The Gift* is also a serious parody. Alexander Yakovlevich Chernyshevski, the father of Yasha and the husband of Alexandra Yakovlevna Chernyshevski (this too is parody, for Yasha is a diminutive of Yakov), calls Fyodor on the telephone. He reads Fyodor the first lines of a review of Fyodor's poems and asks him to visit him that evening so that Fyodor will be able to read all of the review. Fyodor, this budding artist, is excited; and he spends most of his day dreaming, "writing" the review, giving it to the reader, including background to the poems as though the unknown reviewer knew Fyodor's life as well as Fyodor does. This background parallels Nabokov's: there is even the same story in this novel and in *Speak, Memory* of the child, Fyodor-Nabokov, who has, during an illness, a dream vision of his mother's going into a store, purchasing a pencil, and then returning home with the pencil. In both the novel and the memoir the vision becomes an actuality, for the mother does come in with a gigantic Faber pencil used as an advertising display (35).

The "review" is first, then, a study of sources in the sense that a certain life gives birth to a certain group of poems; but we should not assume that Nabokov believes that the function of criticism is to find the sources of an art work. The novel is, once more, about the *development* of the artist and his awarenesses. But the "review" is, second, a joke, a hoax; for, when Fyodor arrives at the Chernyshevskis' apartment, he is greeted by a jocular Alexander Yakovlevich, who, when pointing to a newspaper, is not pointing to the review but to the date, April 1. No review exists except that already done by Fyodor, one which is a parody of all reviews as well as a serious discussion of art.

At this same evening party, Fyodor observes (the point of view in the novel is always deceptive, deliberately shifting, but it is nevertheless always Fyodor's) "the most interesting person in the room" who "sat a little distance apart, by the writing desk, and did not take part in the general conversation. . . . He was a youth somewhat resembling Fyodor . . ." (45). This youth is Yasha Chernyshevski, who, two years dead, has been brought alive by Fyodor because Fyodor is trying to feel his way into the mind of Yasha's father; for Fyodor, an artist, is not just himself, an ego, but any other: "the lighting of the world would suddenly change and for a minute he would actually become Alexander Chernyshevski, or Lyubov Markovna, or Vasiliev" (48).

And, although Fyodor decides that Chernyshevski is not actually imagining his dead son as being there, Fyodor continues to pursue the double life of being at the party as himself and of nevertheless slowly "writing" this biography of Yasha — a biography the mother has asked Fyodor to write after seeing the "similarity" between Fyodor and Yasha. But Fyodor feels no kinship, physical or spiritual, with Yasha, who, for example, admired Spengler, a turgid writer; whose poems are "replete with fashionable clichés"; and who made errors in his Russian as well as in his facts. "I also remember," Fyodor notes, "a rather pathetic reference to 'Vrublyov's frescoes' — an amusing cross between two Russian painters (Rublyov and Vrubel) that only served to prove our dissimilarity: no, he could not have loved painting as I do" (50 - 51). Nonetheless, Fyodor cannot leave Yasha alone until he has fully created him.

As a result, the biography grows in Fyodor's imagination — the story of Yasha and his two fellow students at Berlin University, Rudolf Baumann, who is German, and Olya G., a Russian. They fall in love, a pitiful and parodic triangle: Rudolf with Olya, Olya with Yasha, and Yasha with Rudolf. Yasha's story, though, is not a confession but a multilevel work of art which includes the Nabokovian verbal comedy that is really satire: Rudolf is described as "the son of a respectable fool of a professor and a civil servant's daughter," and he had "grown up in wonderful bourgeois surroundings, between a cathedral-like sideboard and the backs of dormant books" (55).

The three lovers, caught in their neurotic net, decide by almost imperceptible degrees to commit suicide. In the spring of the year — the parody suicide must occur when life is being reborn — they go "on streetcar fifty-seven for the Grunewald where they planned to find a lonely spot and shoot themselves one after the other" (58). But, as we expect, only Yasha kills himself. Nabokov, tying the end of his book to the beginning, casually mentions a certain architect Ferdinand Stockschmeisser who, having been there a while before, departed too early to give help to the survivors; Stockschmeisser reappears some two hundred pages later to talk about the crash of a plane in which two lovers died. That is all; but Stockschmeisser, who only connects but does connect, is brought alive by Nabokov and killed in two separate sentences (the kind of feat Nabokov praises Gogol for). But Yasha, a more interesting artistic problem, must be and is developed so that Fyodor will grow beyond the subjective experience of his poems by becoming more perceptive to the world outside himself.

Therefore Fyodor comes into contact with or at least speaks of other artists — ones from whom he can learn, either by their successes or by their failures. Paintings of the artist Romanov, such as the Nabokov-like "Coincidence" or "Four Citizens Catching a Canary," illustrate connection, hidden objects that are obvious, all things related by mad juxtaposition. And by way of Romanov — that is, by way of his friends, the Lorentzes — the name of Zina Mertz first enters the novel. Her name is casually mentioned, which is Nabokov's way of throwing out a signal that the reader remain forever alert (71). The chapter closes with a literary evening: there is the reading of a play by an utter failure, a man who does not know his Russian or his names — the Greek philosopher Thales becomes Phales. This "error" does not exist in the Russian original, for "Phales" is correct Russian for Thales, although there is no doubt an "unconscious" pun on the Russian word for "phallus." The man has no saving artistic gifts.

Fyodor has a conversation with the poet Koncheyev, the only writer who, Fyodor feels, is his equal, his competitor — and who may be a partial portrait of Khodasevich.[5] In their brilliant, cutting conversation about the history of Russian literature, Fyodor shares all of Nabokov's loves and hates, as well as his belief that the artist must know his tradition — which tells what they think literature should be. But another paradox is that their conversation is imaginary and is Fyodor's wish; for he admires Koncheyev and wants to learn from him: "Whose business is it that actually we [Koncheyev and Fyodor] parted at the very first corner, and that I have been reciting a fictitious dialogue with myself as supplied by a self-teaching handbook of literary inspiration?" (88).

I *Pushkin*

Chapter 2, Nabokov says, "is a surge toward Pushkin in Fyodor's literary progress and contains his attempt to describe his father's zoological explorations" (10). His assertion does not offer much help in interpreting the chapter nor in perceiving its place in the novel's structure until we realize that the bow to Pushkin is not only one to a literary father but also a step in the history of Russian literature and in the creation of the artist. The story of the father's zoological explorations is one more attempt to show how an art work based on an, "actual" life becomes more than sociology.

The chapter begins with a rain that triggers for Fyodor a series of memories of Russia, of his father, of that past which must be worried into shape; and it closes with Fydor's departure from the house he had moved into as the novel begins. Now, in this new move about two years later, "the distance from the old residence to the new was about the same as, somewhere in Russia, that from Pushkin Avenue to Gogol Street" (157) — a distance which indicates more literary history and more learning by the artist. Between that beginning and that ending, then, Fyodor finally comes to terms with his own past; with the father figure(s), actual and artistic; and with his ability to learn from the perhaps artistically more sympathetic Gogol.

The chapter, therefore, is devoted almost completely to the biography of Fyodor's father — the biography which he does not write, and which, once more, is nevertheless written. Fyodor cannot write the biography because he has not been able to escape himself; he is as yet the incomplete novelist. And he still lacks understanding; for, although he loves his father and will hardly love that Chernyshevski whose biography he *will* write, he cannot be objective enough to understand.

Fyodor's father, of course, shares something with Nabokov's father; but their actual lives were very different. What they have in common is an interest in the natural world and, in particular, in butterflies; and their sons share this interest. But Fyodor's father is the complete naturalist, a great collector; he is almost never home; and his family life consists of short episodes between journeys. Instead of being a man of politics, as Nabokov's father was, Fyodor's father has no interest in such things and almost none, in fact, in people. So uninterested in politics is he that he leaves Russia in the closing years of World War I on an exploring trip into remotest Asia. He disappears there, and his final fate remains unreliable rumor.

His wife, like Alexandra Yakovlevna, wants Fyodor to recreate the dead; and, because Fyodor loves his father, he begins work, but not by writing. Instead, he reads Pushkin: "Thus did he hearken to the purest sound from Pushkin's tuning fork — and he already knew exactly what this sound required of him" (108). But "he continued, however, to wait — the planned work was a wafture of bliss, and he was afraid to spoil that bliss by haste and moreover the complex responsibility of the work frightened him" (109). Yet, even in waiting, he is learning. In living with Pushkin, in learning about "the accuracy of the words and the absolute purity of their conjunction" (109), and in seeing Pushkin characters in the people he meets — seeing not the sameness of all men but the human insights of Pushkin — he is making his last step toward the mastery of language and objectivity which will enable him to be a novelist and something other than the subjective poet.

Fyodor also reads other things, such as "the remarkable *Memoirs of the Past* of A. N. Suhoshchokov," which recounts the history of Fyodor's grandfather that Nabokov will use as a basis for his 1944 short story, "A Forgotten Poet." Fyodor's grandfather, having quarreled with his family in 1836, went to Texas where he made a fortune, returning only twenty years later. One evening at the theater, Fyodor's grandfather asks the then young Suhoshchokov whether Pushkin is alive and if he is writing. Suhoshchokov, the joker, replies that Pushkin has just published a new poem; and, pointing to a man in the theater, he asserts that the man is Pushkin. "The act finished; applause thundered. Gray-haired Pushkin stood up abruptly, and still smiling, with a bright sparkle in his youthful eyes, quickly left his box" (113). But Pushkin, of course, had died in a duel in 1837.

Suhoshchokov's "lie" is not only a jokingly serious creation of a double but also a sudden, chilling irruption of the past into the present — and Suhoshchokov is frightened at what he has done. However, past time is mysteriously always with us, especially in art. Suhoshchokov (an invented memoirist, it must be understood) says that Russia will "long continue to feel the living presence of Pushkin"; and he adds that the poet, who extracted "poetry out of his past," found in that past "tragic thoughts about the future. The triple formula of human existence: irrevocability, unrealizability, inevitability — was well known to him" (111). These are the thematic concerns of Fyodor — and they are also the permanent themes of Nabokov. What Pushkin offers, then, is not only "art" in the narrow sense but "art" which is an insight into life.

When Fyodor begins to *think* about the biography of his father, he is recovering the past, first by using his own memories, the memories of his mother, the things he can discover in books, and the memories of other men. But he soon begins to shape the biography himself and to depend no longer upon these externalities. He imagines his father to be on one of his journeys: at first, it is "imaginary" in that Fyodor "visualizes" the journey in his mind's eye, and the reader is told this. Then, almost imperceptibly, Nabokov makes a subtle shift in point of view; the traveler has become two, "he and I"; and Fyodor himself rides with his father through the strange, wild, and beautiful Asian landscape. In a second shift, the "we" is not Fyodor and his

father but the whole party; and the central figure is "I." Fyodor has
been completely identified with the father, the father has become
the son, and the son the father until suddenly "Fyodor saw again the
dead and impossible tulips of his wallpaper" and the recreation is
over (137). Time cannot be denied forever.

This recreation is almost as far as Fyodor can go at this time; but
he writes to his mother with unconscious but complete accuracy that
"at times I feel that somewhere it has already been written by me,
that it is here, hiding in this inky jungle, that I have only to free it
part by part from the darkness and the parts will fall together of
themselves. . . ." And, if he has done that in the novel which he has
not yet written, he has not yet done it because he knows that he is
not yet prepared: he is "afraid I might dirty it with a flashy phrase,
or wear it out in the course of transfer onto paper . . ." (150).

Now he moves from his room in a house run by a German landlady
to one in the apartment of Russian émigrés, the Shchyogolovs —
Mrs. Shchyogolov has a daughter by her first husband, who was
Jewish, named Zina. When Zina at last enters the novel, entering it
with Gogol, she bears with her a gift, for she inspires Fyodor; Fyodor
will at last begin to write something other than his poems.

II *Gogol*

As Nabokov states, the third chapter "shifts to Gogol, but its real
hub is the love poem dedicated to Zina" (10). At moments in the
chapter Fyodor once more becomes "I," and he directly addresses a
"you," Zina (as Nabokov addresses his own wife in *Speak, Memory*).
After an excursus of memory about his first struggles with writing
verse in Russia, Fyodor thinks of his "*Poems*, published two years
ago now," of which only fifty-one copies had ever been sold — one
of them was bought just after publication by the then unknown Zina
Mertz (167). Zina is, therefore, not only Fyodor's love but also as his
audience and his inspiration, part of his growth as artist.

But "to fiction be as to your country true" (168). And if Fyodor,
like Nabokov, must make his living by teaching English to intellectually limited German men or to lonely German women, what he
really wants to teach is the values of the imagination — how it connects, recalls, and plays marvelous, human tricks. Zina encourages
Fyodor in his decision to write the biography of Nikolay Gavrilovich
Chernyshevski about whom Alexander Yakovlevich Chernyshevski
had wanted Fyodor to write "a little book in the form of a *biographie
romancée*" (52). A. Y. Chernyshevski's grandfather, a Jew, had been

converted to Christianity by the priest father of N. G. Chernyshevski
— the real and the fictional once more meet in Nabokov's work —
and so had taken Chernyshevski as a last name. Zina's and Chernyshevski's "Jewishness" joins them together; more important,
Fyodor, the creation of Nabokov was, as Nabokov writes,
"influenced by the rise of a nauseous dictatorship belonging to the
period when the novel was written and not to the one it patchily
reflects" (10). Art is, despite all, influenced by life.

N. G. Chernyshevski was and is a hero to the old-fashioned Russian liberal as well as to more modern radicals. A man of good will, a
relatively mild social radical, Chernyshevski suffered from a cruel
and unfaithful wife and from a cruel and unjust state. But to Fyodor
— and Nabokov — Chernyshevski should be almost an enemy; for
Chernyshevski, a utilitarian, maintained that art's absolute function
is to bring about social change; to him, art is useful but never
autonomous. His concept of art, then, was truly "Platonic"; for, as
D. S. Mirsky points out, Chernyshevski "contended that art, being
nothing but a more or less adequate imitation of reality, is always in-
ferior to the reality it represents."[6] Therefore, when Fyodor is asked
by Alexandra Yakovlevna about why he now wants to write the
biography — Alexander Yakovlevich denies that he has ever asked
Fyodor to do so; truth is shifty — Fyodor replies, "Firing practice"
(208).

Yet, if his motives seem paradoxical, paradox is a necessity for
Fyodor. N. G. Chernyshevski's personal life is not really Fyodor's
concern, although he will be scrupulously exact; it is rather Chernyshevski's artistic influence that must be met and overcome, but
met and overcome on his own grounds of "historical truth." And the
influence will be overcome by making the life into a work of art —
by finding and creating, by following "one of those thematic 'voices'
with which, according to all the rules of harmony, destiny enriches
the life of observant men" (211).

However, since the novel is also a political one, Fyodor must learn
what Chernyshevski represents and, in an odd way, to appreciate
that. He does appreciate Chernyshevski's risks, his courage, and, for
that matter, his goodness; but Fyodor's, and Nabokov's, objections
to the view that art is subject to something other than the imagination apply to all political and moral controls: "in paragraph 146 of
the censorship code for 1826, in which authors were enjoined to
'uphold chaste morals and not to replace them solely by beauty of
the imagination,' one had only to replace 'chaste' by 'civic' or some

such word in order to get the private censorship code of the radical critics . . ." (214). As a result of Fyodor's attitudes, he examines the man, praises him when he can be praised, damns him when necessary, and shows his courage and his stupidity; and, as he does so, the two themes of art and politics make a work of art.

The biography is "in the shape of a ring, closed with the clasp of an apocryphal sonnet (so that the result would be not the form of a book, which by its finiteness is opposed to the circular nature of everything in existence, but a continuously curving, and thus infinite, sentence) . . ." (216). The chapter, then, begins with the sonnet's sestet and ends with its octave. But Fyodor also makes "the end of his work . . . the hero's birth" (217), which is exactly what Nabokov does in his own work on Gogol — although Nabokov loves Gogol.

When Fyodor's biography is finished, he takes it to his friend Vasiliev, the editor of the liberal newspaper, *Gazeta;* and Vasiliev refuses it: "There can be no question of my being party to its publication. I assumed that this was a serious work, and it turns out to be a reckless, antisocial, mischievous improvisation" (219). We must remember Nabokov's remark about the book's being published in *Sovremennye Zapiski* without that same chapter and for the same reasons the liberal Vasiliev gives: one does not attack a good man, a liberal hero, since doing so is personally and socially evil. But the biography is not an attack on the man; it *is* accurate. It is concerned with a "deeper truth," as Zina knows, and with one for which Fyodor "alone was responsible and which he alone could find." This truth "was for her so important that the least clumsiness or fogginess in his words seemed to be the germ of a falsehood, which had to be immediately exterminated" (217). Truth differs from propaganda, which is flat and so untrue.

Fyodor does find his publisher and the work gets printed — and it is regarded by the man who helps in its publication as "a good slap at Marxism (to the delivery of which Fyodor had not given the least thought when writing his work) . . ." (223), a statement that we must take with more than a grain of salt, but one which does reinforce the idea that art in itself is not tendentious.

III *The Biography*

Chapter 4 is, then, the story of N. G. Chernyshevski (1828 - 1889). A fascinating biography, it is based on the documents; and the only "imagined" part is that a certain biographer of Chernyshevski,

Strannolyubski ("Strangelove,"), who makes some of the more insightful and witty remarks about Chernyshevski's life, is Fyodor-Nabokov's invention. The autobiography finds the connections, the fatidic dates, that Nabokov loves: the wedding of Chernyshevski's best friend — with whose wife Chernyshevski falls in love before his own marriage — takes place sixteen years to the day before Chernyshevski's "civil execution," that ceremonial rite by which, with an incised sword broken over his neck, he is symbollically killed, deprived of all civil existence in Russia, and sent to Siberian exile.

For the educated Russian reader, there would be little that is new in the biography in the sense that there are no startling factual matters. For the American reader, an acquaintance with a straight biography, as well as some reading in the history of mid-nineteenth-century Russia, might be helpful in seeing what Nabokov has done. For Fyodor's (Nabokov's) strikingly original work makes Chernyshevski a truly sympathetic, if foolish, man and rescues him from politics in the sense that he becomes human and not a symbol. And with that feat, Fyodor, having created another human being, can become the novelist he was born to be.

IV *The Resolution of Themes*

The final chapter of *The Gift* "combines," Nabokov says, "all the preceding themes and adumbrates the book Fyodor dreams of writing some day: The Gift" (10). The chapter begins with the reactions to Fyodor's book, but only one review really comprehends the work — the one by Koncheyev. As a result, we get the second conversation with Koncheyev about art; and Koncheyev tells Fyodor both what is good in his writing and what is bad. In this criticism we must see not only Fyodor's new ability to criticize himself but also Nabokov's self-appraisal. The defects, Koncheyev says, are

first, an excessive trust in words. . . . Secondly, there is a certain awkwardness in the reworking of the sources: You seem to be undecided whether to enforce your style upon past speeches and events or to make their own more salient. . . . Thirdly, you sometimes bring up parody to such a degree of naturalness that it actually becomes a genuine serious thought, but on *this* level it suddenly falters, lapsing into a mannerism that is yours and not a parody of a mannerism. . . . Fourthly, one observes in one or two of your transitions something mechanical, if not automatic. . . . Fifthly and finally, you sometimes say things chiefly calculated to prick your contemporaries. . . . The real writer should ignore all readers but one, that of the future, who in his turn is merely the author reflected in time. (351 - 52)

This conversation is like the first one, imaginary; and Fyodor never does talk to Koncheyev, nor for that matter with the novelist Vladimirov — who looks like Nabokov and who "at twenty-nine . . . was already the author of two novels — outstanding for the force and swiftness of their mirror-like style — which irritated Fyodor perhaps for the very reason that he felt a certain affinity with him" (333). The affinity is almost doubleness.

But Fyodor has been able, through his work, to come to terms with his past and with himself; he now dreams that his father has returned; and for a moment, a kind of hysterical happiness occurs in the book. With Fyodor's awakening, he recognizes that he must and can live through himself, not others. The novel closes with Fyodor and Zina, after having talked about the book he will later write, on their way to the empty apartment where they will spend their first night together alone. But there is one last joke: the keys are locked inside the apartment; and these keys are elements in the image pattern of the novel. Therefore the last words in the narrative are not of love but of art; for the final paragraph, in both Russian and English, is a version of the *Eugene Onegin* stanza of Pushkin. This paragraph says good-bye to the book but suggests that it will continue, that art moves in time by being out of time, but that art is truly our best way of at least holding at bay irrevocability, unrealizability, and inevitability.

CHAPTER 6

The Essential Themes in a New Language

I The Real Life of Sebastian Knight

NOVELIST Sebastian Knight, the title figure of Nabokov's first English novel, *The Real Life of Sebastian Knight*, is discovered lying on the floor just after having finished his second novel; and he looks up at his visitor and announces, "I'm not dead. I have finished building a world, and this is my Sabbath rest."[1] Of Sebastian, V., the narrator of the novel says that time for him "was never 1914 or 1920 or 1936 — it was always year 1" (65). Sebastian himself causes one of his characters, a very autobiographical character, to assert: "There is only one real number: One. And love, apparently, is the best exponent of this singularity" (113).

Sebastian Knight was written in 1938 when the Nabokovs, husband, wife, and four-year-old son, were living in an apartment with one room — plus a small kitchen and a bathroom — in Paris, to which they had escaped from Germany. Nabokov used the bathroom as his writing studio. But the novel, elegant and convoluted despite its lapses, hardly echoes the circumstances of its writing. The work is, to borrow Conrad Brenner's words, "in a vagrant sense . . . Nabokov's contribution to the literature of identity." But the search for identity is not the search for the effects of poverty. The novel is, rather, as Brenner observes, "an outright literary trick, finely woven deceit."[2] What Nabokov is doing in this immediate successor to *Dar*, but in a new and not yet thoroughly obedient language — and what the quotation demonstrates which begins this chapter — is to continue his examination of the essential themes of that final Russian novel: what is art, how is it made, and how does it become part of human life, life which is always in space and time and utterly unpredictable, always escaping art? *Sebastian* lacks the richness of characterization and the complexity of language of *Dar*

and of Nabokov's succeeding English works; but, if it is a minor
Nabokov novel, it is still an excellent one.

Sebastian is not, to repeat, Nabokov; but that he speaks in part for
Nabokov is plain enough. In this respect, we may once more quote
V. who remarks that Sebastian "had a queer habit of endowing even
his most grotesque characters with this or that idea, or impression, or
desire which he himself might have toyed with" (114). Although we
may not agree that Nabokov puts his "ideas" into his own novel in
order to undermine that work, as Brenner asserts, we must
nevertheless agree with Brenner that Nabokov appears "everywhere
on its pages without seeming to appear at all. . . . ."[3] Sebastian shares,
therefore, with his creator those things that allow Nabokov to make
his world. Like Nabokov, Sebastian claims his novels have no
political meanings; like Nabokov, he is insistent upon the value of
the lonely individual; like Nabokov, he is, as V. says, filled with
nostalgia for a lost world, lost time (26 - 27). This novel about Sebastian is, then, about his creator's values — not only those of art and
time, but of love. Nevertheless, unlike Nabokov, Sebastian in his
own life is a rather cold, sometimes unfeeling man — he is not insensitive, but he is distant, an aspect of the artist who remains objective.

As the novel opens, Sebastian Knight is two months dead: born
December 31, 1899, in St. Petersburg, Russia, he died in the small
town of St. Damier, France, in January, 1936. "Damier" is the
French for "chessboard," so that, with "knight," we have yet
another connection between creator and creation and see the artist
tying all worlds together. In between these dates, Sebastian's life has
been devoted to his art and to the one woman he has almost against
his will passionately loved. But the novel is not a chronological
narrative: it is, rather, the search for the facts, as well as the meaning, of Knight's life by his half-brother, V., who acts out of a sense of
duty — and of love. The structure of the novel is not the "story," it is
the story; and the reader must, as Charles Nicol cogently argues,
follow the method as a reader that Nabokov

employs as a writer: seeing the entire novel simultaneously, as numerous
structures, interlocking syllogisms which may proceed in reverse as well as
forward order. For example, Sebastian's experience visiting what he wrongly
believes to be the house his mother died in becomes significant only after V.
has a similar experience — one that leads to the triumphant, visionary an-
nouncement at the end of the novel — while visiting the wrong sickroom.[4]

Therefore, if the novel opens in the pattern of the classic novel,
with V. giving us Sebastian's birthdate and closes with his death, the

novel really takes place in a constant "present." As a result, the emphasis is not, then, upon Sebastian but rather upon V. as he attempts to discover the truth about Sebastian in a search which he compares, quite rightly and quite literally, to "Chichikov's round of weird visits in Gogol's 'Dead Souls' " (143). We are in a Gogolian world in which strange monsters, smiling with human faces, meet us at the door.

Six years younger than Sebastian, V. hardly knew his half-brother even when they were children. They lived together only until they and V.'s mother fled Russia in 1919; after that date, V. saw Sebastian only at long intervals and for only a few hours each time. During such meetings, they never really communicated; therefore, whatever V. learns of Sebastian's later life, he must learn from his search among the friends, acquaintances, and enemies of Sebastian, all unsure sources. V. is on more secure ground about Sebastian's childhood; but even then much of his knowledge is hearsay. One certain thing is that Sebastian, V., and Nabokov all shared the same Swiss governess, and another certainty is that V. and Nabokov visit her in Switzerland long afterward *(Speak, Memory,* Chapter Five; *Sebastian Knight,* p. 21). Sebastian's mother, the Englishwoman Virginia Knight, was the first wife of their father, an upperclass and honorable Russian. Virginia, neurotic and rich, betrayed her husband and left both him and the child Sebastian in a Paris hotel "as suddenly as a rain-drop starts to slide tipwards down a syringa leaf" (a repeated image in Nabokov's work). Her desertion leads Sebastian to remember the day and the hotel room as "a queer expansion of time, time gone astray, asprawl . . ." (9).

Sebastian's father soon remarried, this time a Russian woman; and the marriage seemed to V., the only child of this second marriage, to have been a happy one. Virginia reappeared one more time where she visited Sebastian, for a few minutes only, in 1908; and she died of a heart disease the next year. And so V., both as boy and as man, cannot quite understand why, in 1912, and long after her death, his father, with a strange sense of honor perhaps, or perhaps because he is still in love with Virginia, challenged the man who had run away with her, not for that act but for gossiping about her. In the ensuing duel, the father is killed.

The death of his father in defense of the name of this mother whom Sebastian hardly knew has an overwhelming effect on him. He identifies with his mother, with her country, and with her language to such an extent that, after his escape from Russia, he goes to England and makes himself over into an Englishman. He even calls himself Knight, rather than by the Russian name that he and V. share but one which is never given; for the search for truth is indeed the search for identity. Although Sebastian becomes an English author — in the process, he attends Cambridge, just as Nabokov did — he is in his heart always a Russian. (It is not by chance that Virginia and Sebastian are associated with violets, with blue, with Nabokov's color.) In fact, at the end of Sebastian's life, he reverts to the Russian language when he writes V. a letter; to his Russian name; and, therefore, to his Russian being, his identity.

In the middle 1920s, Sebastian meets the girl Clare Bishop; but V. learns about them only through an accidental encounter in Paris. We cannot be quite sure of her name since Sebastian introduces her to V. as "Miss Bishop"; afterward, when V. meets the man she marries after Sebastian has abandoned her, that man announces, "My name is Bishop . . ." (77). Sebastian's and Clare's life together is calm: she is both his lover and his collaborator, and with her he completes his first two novels and a collection of short stories. He is, we can assume, as happy, and as much the artist, as he will ever be.

But time cannot be escaped. Having discovered that he is suffering from the same heart disease that killed his mother, he follows his doctor's advice and goes for treatment to the spa at Blauberg (one more "blue" mountain) in Alsace. He goes alone, and there he meets the Russian woman who makes the rest of his short life utterly miserable. The artist cannot escape the human.

This information about the woman V. pieces together from several sources, but his "discovery" of her depends upon a chance meeting (one more accident, one more act of fate) with a little, multilingual, multinational ex-policeman who gets the necessary information for him, asks nothing in return, and then disappears utterly — indeed, a *deus ex machina*, who is a satire upon gods from machines but who is nevertheless a charming man.

The woman's original name, so far as we can know any truth of fact in the novel, was Nina Toovoretz; when Sebastian knew her, she was Madame "de" Rechnoy; and V. meets her under the name of Lecerf. V. does not know, at first, that she is the woman for whom he is searching; she pretends to be only a friend of the Helene von Graun whom V. believes is the woman he has been seeking. But she knows a man who can write his name upside down and reveals this fact — and V. has already met the man. We must point out, though, that V. never directly makes the connection for the reader; the reader must remember and associate two distant remarks by himself.

The woman does not love Sebastian, although for a little while she is interested in him, perhaps because he is a kind of challenge. However, after she has played with him and caused him intense pain, she gets thoroughly bored and sends one of her other male admirers to tell Sebastian that she will not see him again. Not too long after this incident, he dies, alone, in the little hospital in St. Damier. V., having received a telegram from Sebastian's doctor, hurries there and even spends a few minutes in a small room, one adjoining what he believes to be his brother's room, listening to his brother breathe: and "that gentle breathing was telling me more of Sebastian than I had ever known before. If I could have smoked, my happiness would have been perfect" (203). Only after leaving the room does V. learn that there has been a mistake; under his Russian name, his brother had died the night before. The irony is heavy.

This, then, is the story line; but since most of the novel is devoted to V.'s actual search, the real characters are the people he meets who tell him about Sebastian; and the real structure is the interlocking not only of the two stories but of all the particulars of those two stories. Sebastian's own works, therefore, are not only included in but also include the novel we are reading, for they are Sebastian's and Nabokov's. At one and the same time, they are works of art and parodies of a certain kind of art; indeed, they are self-parodies. In passing, we should observe that Sebastian, like Nabokov, "belonged to that rare type of writer who knows that nothing ought to remain except the perfect achievement: the printed book"; therefore, Sebastian destroys all notes and drafts (36).

But Sebastian's works are also about the world; for V. says of Sebastian's first two novels that, "if . . . [the] first . . . is based on methods of literary composition, — the second one deals mainly with the methods of human fate" (95). The emphasis may be upon the word "methods," but methods must deal with matter. Sebastian's first novel is *The Prismatic Bezel*, a properly enigmatic title. Sebastian had once considered calling it *Cock Robin Hits Back*, a half-joke title which Clare, in V.'s presence, attacks by asserting that "a title . . . must convey the colour of the book, — not its subject" (72). The novel's subject is, to say the least, excruciatingly banal; it is a very British murder mystery. The action takes place in a boardinghouse; there are twelve boarders; and all the survivors become suspects when one of them, G. Abeson, is murdered. We find not only the standard stupid policeman but also the usual exposure of dark secrets in the lives of everyone of the suspects, all of whom have some hidden connection with one or more of the others. However, "a new plot, a new drama utterly unconnected with the opening of the story, which is thus thrust back into the region of dreams, seems to struggle for existence and break into light" (94). This new "drama" flashes momentarily before the reader when the novel resolves itself: G. Abeson, still alive, turns out to be the mild old man, Nosebag, who has wandered into the boardinghouse; and no murder has occurred.

Nabokov might never have written Sebastian's novel, even though he has, as he did Fyodor Godunov-Cherdyntsev's works; but his own novel is performing the same bewildering trick by presenting another subject under his apparent one. *The Prismatic Bezel* is, as V. says, Sebastian's way of using "parody as a kind of springboard for leaping into the highest region of serious emotion" (91). It is Sebastian's attack on that solemn hypocrisy and fakery which Nabokov, in his book on Gogol, characterizes by the Russian word *poshlust:* "the obviously trashy but also the falsely important, the falsely beautiful, the falsely clever, the falsely attractive."[5] Such "shamming" is, V. asserts, "in an *artistic* sense, immoral." Therefore, "*The Prismatic Bezel* is not only a rollicking parody of the setting of a detective tale; it is also a wicked imitation of many other things . . . , namely the fashionable trick of grouping a medley of people in a limited space (a hotel, an island, a street). Then also different kinds of styles are satirized. . . . But all this obscure fun is . . . only the author's springboard" (92).

Sebastian's second novel, *Success,* is even more the exemplar and yet the parody of Nabokov's own work as well as the work of others — of indulgers in *poshlust* as well as of true artists. The structure of the novel is almost the structure of *Sebastian Knight:* "a certain commercial traveller Percival Q. at a certain stage of his life and in certain circumstances meets the girl, a conjuror's assistant, with whom he will be happy ever after." But the figure of the conjuror, as noted above, is a constant in Nabokov's works; for the conjuror is the trickster whose tricks, which fool us, are nevertheless patently tricks; they are honest and brilliant. And it is so with Sebastian's novel; for, although the meeting of Percival Q. and the girl seems accidental, "all the magic and force of . . . [the author's] art are summoned in order to discover the exact way in which two lines of life were made to come into contact . . ." (96). Percival and the girl have almost met before, just as Zina and Fyodor in *The Gift* nearly meet again and again before they really do. "But fate is much too persevering to be put off by failure" (98); and since they are at last brought together, the novel seems to be playing with the concept of our being held in the hands of fate. But we must remember that the novel is not experience in itself, not life; it is a structure for a purpose perhaps, but nevertheless a structure.

Therefore, the structure of *Success* is dependent upon the author's following all the clues which will lead us back to the present — and this artistic "detective" work is, of course, what V. does, while attempting to discover the truth about Sebastian. In this way, Sebastian's life is examined not just as a "parody" of the *biographie romancée* — "the worst kind of literature" (20), V. says, agreeing with Nabokov and Fyodor. This work is not only a parody of the novel about the search for identity — with the parodic doubleness of not only satirizing the genre but taking it seriously at the same moment — but also a parody of certain literary character types who represent aspects of human behavior, even if the critic is not willing to agree that they are truly human.

The parody of character types begins with Mr. Goodman, who was Sebastian's "secretary" and who publishes a biographical-critical study, a *biographie romancée*, of Sebastian called *The Tragedy of Sebastian Knight,* a book which V. rather nastily points out "has enjoyed a very good press," being "called 'impressive and convincing.' The author has been credited with 'deep insight' into an 'essentially modern' character" (61). These clichés Nabokov regards as utterly damning; and the person whose work calls forth such adjectives is likely to be no better than his work. Indeed, Goodman is a dreadful bore who denigrates Sebastian, first, because Sebastian is — and this judgment is, I think, to be accepted — a good writer, and, second, because Goodman's concept of art is not only anti-art but, in the end, antihuman. Goodman's "sole object is to show 'poor Knight' as a product and victim of what he calls 'our time' . . ." (62); or, as Goodman himself phrases his objective, he wishes to demonstrate the "fatal split between Knight the artist and the great booming world about him. . . ." Knight's "aloofness is a cardinal sin in an age when a perplexed humanity eagerly turns to its writers and thinkers, and demands of them attention to, if not the cure of, its woes and wounds . . ." (117).

For Goodman, therefore, art must have only a moral purpose, a social purpose; in the end, by denying art any existence in itself, he is denying the artist his right to be free, to be individual, not only as a producer but as a man. It is a pleasure, then, to have V., after his interview with Goodman, say, "Mr. Goodman's large soft pinkish face was, and is, remarkably like a cow's udder" (60). Art can be, with Nabokov, satire.

Madam Lecerf, Madame de Rechnoy, or Nina Toovoretz is unlike Goodman: she is intelligent, beautiful and charming. But she lacks human feeling. Of course, she should be less charming and more strident in order to fit exactly the type she is parodying, the female vampire; but, in this limited sense, Nabokov's people are never what they should be. It is true that, as with Sebastian, what we know about Nina is learned largely through the reports of others — and, in the last analysis, from V. As I have noted, she does appear finally and gives us information about Sebastian and herself while pretending to be a friend of the woman Sebastian loved. She suggests in this roundabout, devious way that she had really loved only one man, a married man who rejected her, and that whatever happened afterward with other men was a kind of play. In this sense, Sebastian is a victim of another person's life.

Nina's former husband, Paul Rechnoy (the "de" is her affectation), says: "She's not a girl you can easily forget once she's got into your system. She sucked me dry, and in more ways than one. Money and soul, for instance." And, he adds, "Her idea of life was drinking cocktails, and eating a large supper at four o'clock in the morning, and dancing the shimmy . . . , and inspecting brothels because that was fashionable . . . , and buying expensive clothes, and raising hell in hotels . . ." (145 - 46). Of such a person, V. quite rightly says, unknowingly to the woman herself, that "I am at a loss to imagine how such a woman could attract my brother . . ." (161). She has just said of Sebastian that "he was a difficult sort of man" and that her "friend" "liked his looks and his hands and his manner of talking, and she thought it would be rather good fun to have him make love to her — because, you see, he looked so very intellectual, and it is always entertaining to see that kind of refined, distant, — brainy fellow suddenly go on all fours and wag his tail" (158 - 59).

But Sebastian "did not turn into a sentimental pup, as she had expected," Madame Lecerf adds. Yet he loved her, condemned her, fought against her, and succumbed to her again and again, even intending his last letter for her, before, in midparagraph, he changed it to V. What attracted him to her is never explained, and deliberately so: her beauty, charm, and intelligence are insufficient reasons since her character and her personality should have repelled Sebastian. We could argue that Sebastian sees his mother in her, that cold, distant woman whom he idolized. The mother is continually associated with violets, with blue — it is no chance then that V., before he decides to write Sebastian's biography, destroys unread, because Sebastian wished it, letters from the unknown beloved that were written on "note paper [that] was egg-shell blue with a dark-blue rim" (38). Later, when V. meets the woman, he notes the "blueish sheen to her hair," the "blue vein on her pale girlish neck," and "violet dark eyelids" (165, 168, 171). And this association is not a kind of Freudianizing but a Nabokovianizing, for the connections are there.

The making of and finding of connections are, of course, the act of the artist as he attempts to order and understand his world. "All things belong to the same order of things, for such is the oneness of human perception, the oneness of individuality, the oneness of matter, whatever matter may be. The only real number is one, the rest are mere repetition" (105). Sebastian had written this statement in *Lost Property,* "his most autobiographical work" (26). He began to write this novel at the Beaumont Hotel in Blauberg where he met Nina. And in this novel he says also, "There is only one real number: One. And love, apparently, is the best exponent of this singularity" (113). Although, and because, "time and space were to him measures of the same eternity" (66), as V. remarks, what V. is left with is a mystery. V. passes through the same experiences that the dying central figure has in Sebastian's *The Doubtful Asphodel,* for this character thinks that soon "everything would be unravelled, — everything that he might imagine in our childish terms of space and time, both being riddles invented by man *as* riddles, and thus coming back at us: the boomerangs of nonsense. . . ." But, at the end, "the author seems to pause for a minute," and in "that minute of doubt . . . the man is dead," the "absolute solution" of existence has been lost — although V. thinks that the solution is hidden, "somewhere, concealed in some passage I have read too hastily, or . . . intertwined with other words whose familiar guise deceived me" (178 - 80). But the artist does not give us the solution; he opens up the mystery.

As the book nears its close, V. muses: "The end, the end. They all go back to their everyday life (and Clare goes back to her grave) — but the hero remains, for, try as I may, I cannot get out of my part: Sebastian's mask clings to my face, the likeness will not be washed off. I am Sebastian, or Sebastian is I, or perhaps we both are someone whom neither of us knows" (205). V. is Sebastian as Sebastian is V. — in the sense that V. has created Sebastian in this biography, just as V. and Sebastian are Nabokov, that "someone whom neither of" them knows. Once again, if a mystery lies at the center of human existence, the ambiguities of human love and of artistic creation are the only means of exploring that mystery. And yet "the mystery remains intact," as Nabokov says in "An Evening of Russian Poetry."

II Bend Sinister

The Real Life of Sebastian Knight and *Bend Sinister*, Nabokov's first two novels in English, are relatively unknown but undeservedly so. Although they are lesser novels than *Lolita* and *Pale Fire*, they are always interesting. *Bend Sinister* tells a fascinating story that continues Nabokov's themes. Although the novel is neither quite history nor an allegory of history, it is Nabokov's most explicitly political novel in that it deals most concretely with living political themes. In *Conclusive Evidence*, Nabokov observes that *Invitation to a Beheading*, written in the previous decade, treats "the buffoons and bullies of a Communazist state."[6] He also says in his foreword to the translated *Invitation* that this novel and *Bend Sinister* are related stylistically, which means thematically. They are both visions of madness, political and personal. Madness occurs when the individual begins to act in the world as though his dreams were actual — and this kind of action is a perversion of the artistic act.

But other equally important themes appear in *Bend Sinister*. What we might consider the positive message of the novel is contained in the statement of Krug, the philosopher protagonist, when he says that he esteems his university colleagues because they experience "perfect felicity in specialized knowledge" and are unlikely to commit murder.[7] In other words, there are human values which must be upheld against those mad abstractions which, as we shall see, would destroy the mind and the body by treating man as only a machine.

Yet, as Nabokov announces, he neither writes nor reads "didactic fiction."[8] For "great literary achievements . . . [are phenomena] of language and not . . . of ideas."[9] And once more we do not need to take his statement entirely seriously. His own creature, Sebastian Knight, puts this last statement in reverse order and makes it more accurate by asserting "that no real idea can be said to exist without the words made to measure."[10] *Bend Sinister* is an example of how words are made to measure a political idea; but the novel is also concerned with words themselves and, therefore, with literature — literature is the dream of the artist, a dream that makes nothing happen but just *is*.

The novel, however, is not these generalizations; it is a construction of words, but it is also a story about people in a world. The action takes place in an unnamed but obviously modern European country, somewhere east of France: a revolution, led by Paduk, has just overthrown the Republic and Paduk has become dictator. As the novel begins, Krug, the hero, leaves the hospital where his wife has died. Crossing a bridge, he has a hallucinatory encounter with the soldiers of the insane dictator; and this event is representative of those that follow. Krug talks himself past the soldiers on the north side of the bridge, but he is turned back at the south because his pass has not been signed at the other end. The soldiers on the north side, one of whom is Gurk ("Krug" spelled backwards), are illiterate. In brief, Krug does not exist as a person until he can get a signature from people who cannot write. Finally, he and another man, who is also held up, sign each other's passes — a nice irony; for the two prisoners create each other as persons, through written words, and so escape.

Krug and Paduk had been schoolmates as children; and Paduk's new state wants Krug's endorsement for propaganda reasons, although there is an overtone of homosexuality in Paduk's desire for Krug's approval. It would not be an over-reading to interpret Paduk's implied homosexuality as a personal and political commentary: the dictator, the seeker for power (an essentially sterile personality), lusts after the life of the mind at the same moment that he needs to degrade it. Since Krug wishes to retain his individuality, he refuses to endorse the regime. "I want to be left alone," he says (91); and, too, "I am not interested in politics" (5). There is a moral lesson here: he should be interested in politics. For, one by one, his friends, people of no political importance, are dragged to prison as a kind of blackmail; and, at last, his own young son is taken. Krug collapses and is willing to do and sign anything; human love is the highest value. "The nightmare may get out of control," Krug cries to a state functionary (211). Unfortunately, it does; and his son is killed in a brutal psychological "experiment." Krug, now insane, believes himself to be a schoolchild again, attacks Paduk, and is shot.

Paduk is the chief advocate of Ekwilism, a "violent and virulent political doctrine" that proposes "to enforce spiritual uniformity upon . . . [the] land through the medium of the most standardized section of the inhabitants, namely the Army, under the supervision of a bloated and dangerously divine State" (76). Nabokov presents Ekwilism as a basically confused political idea with one clear aim: destruction of the individual. Communist and Nazi dogma — racism, militarism, extreme nationalism — seem to be casually included; but there is more Nazi, perhaps, than Communist doctrine in this list. Moreover, the emblem of the Ekwilist state resembles "a crushed dislocated but still writhing spider" (34). Displayed on a red background, this figure is an obvious mimic of the Nazi swastika and banner, although it contains an echo of the red flag. And Krug, certainly ironically, asks the unlettered soldiers to sign his pass with "a cross . . . or a gammadion, or something" (15). The gammadion can be in the shape of a swastika and, possibly not too oddly, of an open-ended Greek cross. The swastika, in German, is a *hakenkreuz*, a hook-cross; but the Christian cross has also been used as a symbol by killers.

As I have noted before, however, Nabokov, in pursuing the image of the circle which is so important to his art, sees the figure of the political circle joining, "a vicious circle as all circles are."[11] The death of the heart, "spiritual uniformity," is the result, if not the purpose, of both Communism and Nazism. The *petit bourgeois* who does sign Krug's pass is, in his emptiness, as vicious as any revolutionist of Paduk's kind; *Bend Sinister* must not be read as an apologia for capitalism. Nabokov gives the circle explicit meaning in *Speak, Memory*, when he suggests that a kind of circle links "representatives of all nations" — imperialists, French policemen, Nazis, Russian and Polish inciters of pogroms, American lynchers, racists, and, finally, the expressionless, insensitive "automatons" who are the products of Russian Communism.[12] This image of the circle is, therefore, the "illogical" truth of the dream: it shows us how apparently dissimilar political ideals are really and not just superficially identical.

Above all, Ekwilism is and must be opposed to the life of the mind. As an acquaintance of Krug maintains (repeating Krug's thought), "Curiosity . . . is insubordination in its purest form" (44). Ekwilism would destroy curiosity (any search for truth); but a lower kind of curiosity, the impulse to pry into other people's business, is made a virtue. Ekwilism would certainly destroy art, at least art as Nabokov understands it; for "Popular commonsense must spit out the caviar of moonshine and poetry, and the simple word, *verbum sine ornatu*, intelligible to man and beast [!] alike, and accompanied by fit action, must be restored to power" (110). These senselessly fumbled but frightening metaphors with their accent on action, an action that can mean only violence, are the language of the Ekwilist state — and the antithesis of art and artist. Not too surprisingly, this quoted sentence and part of the description of Shakespeare's Fortinbras in *Hamlet*, which Nabokov gives to his Professor Hamm, are inspired variants of an actual sentence and certain remarks of Franz Horn, a nineteenth-century German commentator on *Hamlet*. I should add that Nabokov borrows from a number of Shakespeare's commentators, many more than I have room to point out (see Horn, et al., in the Furness Variorum *Hamlet*). Under the Ekwilist regime, there will be no more free and yet ordered magical dance of words. The totalitarian, utilitarian mind — not Nabokov's art, not Krug's thought — is what Krug's friend Maximov cries out against: "But the utterly nonsensical is a natural and logical part of Paduk's rule" (89).

The very form of Nabokov's novel is an actualization of this ironic strain between art and politics. Form here means style, structure, and imagery — the three elements of literary work which, in the epilogue to *Lolita*,[13] Nabokov suggests are the truly important ones. It is almost impossible, however, to speak of the one without speaking of the other two in his fiction. We cannot, for instance, explain those digressions that really do not digress — those digressions that Nabokov thinks of, along with Laurence Sterne, as "the sun-shine . . . the life, the soul of reading"[14] — without noting that they are imagistically interrelated with the other parts of the novel — and the style changes but makes, too, its correspondences. Nevertheless, we must see how these things work in order to understand that the novel does have order and meaning.

The novel's beginning and its ending offer us examples of Nabokov's use of imagery. The first chapter is apparently set within the mind of Krug, but we cannot be certain. It is November: the observer sees a street; a peculiar, spatulate puddle; two leafless poplar trees; and two houses. The puddle will appear again when the police spy, Dr. Alexander, signs his acquiescence to the State philosophy and accidentally blots the paper. And, almost at the end of the novel — just as Krug rushes across the courtyard at Paduk who is crouched against a wall, and just before Krug is shot dead — the author's voice, an "I," suddenly interrupts, and breaks off the story of Krug. The "I" stretches himself among the scattered pages of the novel he has just finished writing (240 - 41). It is night; the "I" looks out upon two lighted windows; they are the windows in one of the houses seen by "Krug" in the first scene. There is also a poplar and "a special puddle (the one Krug had somehow perceived through the layer of his own life). . . ." The season is different; it is warm and there are moths about, "a good night for mothing" for Nabokov the lepidopterist. Yet Krug and the author are certainly identified; and of that puddle, always "acquiring the same form," the "I" says that, "possibly, something of the kind may be said to occur in regard to the imprint we leave in the intimate texture of space" (241 - 42). The puddle is Krug's, Alexander's, the "I's"; they all share the same space. The author as God is god of a pantheistic world; the dreamer is his own creation.

The novel's structure emphasizes the same themes: the beginning and the end of the novel contain each other as well as the novel. But we must still examine the actual line of the story. I have said that the digressions are not really digressions — and there are admittedly times when Nabokov indulges himself. But the longest of the digressions, the Shakespearean one, is not only a functional but an absolutely necessary part of the novel — it is the assertion of the value of literature. And one element of literature is the sheer joy of using or seeing words used intelligently and sensitively.

The figure of Shakespeare enters the novel early: Krug's friend Ember is translating him; and Krug and Ember entertain the absurd, marvelous fancy of "forging" his works. Shakespeare is important to Nabokov not only because he is, with Pushkin, one of the greatest poets,[15] not only because he is the author of the "dream-plays *Hamlet* . . . [and] *Lear*,"[16] and not only because of the complexity and mystery of his plays, but also because he is a magnificent enigma in himself — a puzzling trickster who hides and reveals himself in his works. The point is that Shakespeare's works are the *type* of literature: the poet, or rather, his works are truly "not of an age, but for all time." They are outside of time; in fact, if Shakespeare did not exist, we should have to invent him for our own time. Krug and Ember can invent him, make him meaningful for themselves as individuals. But we shall see that there is a wrong way of "inventing" him, one that is an assault on language and literature.

The digression about Shakespeare, which takes most of Chapter 7, opens with a partial description of Ember's bedroom. Once again we cannot be sure who is doing the perceiving, Krug, Ember, or the author. Who, for instance, says, "Last chance of describing the bedroom"? (108). The literary dream will not allow us esthetic distance: the voice of the dreamer is at our ear, perhaps *in* our ear. On one wall there are three pictures, all of which have something to do with the Bacon-Shakespeare nonsense. Nabokov does not so inform us, but the first two pictures are derived from the title page of *Cryptomenytices, etc.*, published at Lunaeburg in 1624 as the work of a Gustavus Selenus. One of the English Baconians, Sir Edwin Durning-Lawrence, used Selenus' book to "prove" that Bacon wrote Shakespeare's plays (I have been unable to discover where the third picture comes from).

Sir Edwin's own book, *Bacon is Shakespeare*, offers quite a bit more to Nabokov, including the statement that the Droeshout portrait from the 1623 folio "is cunningly composed of two left arms and a mask."[17] Nabokov modifies this statement as: "Who is he? William X, cunningly composed of two left arms and a mask. Who else? The person who said (not for the first time) that the glory of God is to hide a thing, and the glory of man is to find it" (107). We could argue that Nabokov is simply playing a game with us; he says of Pushkin that he is "a deceiver as all artists are. . . ."[18] Nabokov does not, indeed, take the Bacon-as-Shakespeare faith seriously; to him, Shakespeare is Shakespeare, the "Warwickshire fellow" (107). All this Shakespeare material is, I agree, a joke; but it is more than a joke and more than just an opportunity for Nabokov to make some obscure allusions.

On the immediate level, the Shakespeare discussion serves as a psychological relief for Krug and Ember: Olga, Krug's wife, has just died; and the Maximovs have just been arrested. It is also "comic relief," or, better, a relaxation that heightens the horror of both the Maximovs' arrest in the preceding chapter and the following, weirdly farcical, arrest of Ember. But neither use justifies either the absurdity or the length of the digression which is, in design, neither a wandering nor a psychological manipulation of the reader; instead, it is an enrichment, an attempt on the part of the author to reach out and gather in as much (even if fantastic) life as possible; it is also an attempt to use "language" as effectively as possible. We must also see that these seemingly irrelevant bits of knowledge, these puzzles, these creations of new worlds, are always in the main flow of the novel. They are, to use Pnin's words, "Rambling Comparisons";[19] but, just as the metaphor or the figure makes poetry, so do these digressions make the novel. They are not just baroque ornaments; they connect, and they comment.

Nabokov's borrowings, allusions, and images in the digressions (and elsewhere) work in the same way. Sir Edwin is used because he too has invented "Shakespeare" — but he has done so stupidly, without humor, and with a flawed language; therefore, his is the dream of literature and truth gone sour. In addition, he offers an image with his insistence on Bacon's "left-handedly" putting out his "Shakespeare" plays. The left hand, or the idea of the left or "sinister," appears repeatedly. The title of the novel refers to the band running from sinister chief to dexter base on the shield, a "standard" representation of bastardy in heraldry. It is not that Bacon fathered Shakespeare's plays, but rather that the true work of art contains the world, the left as well as the right; it contains contraries that are dialectically related. Moreover, like questions of parentage, the work of literature contains mysteries. We might add that Nabokov's digressions are a deliberately bizarre interweaving of the comic and the serious, an echo of Shakespeare's practice in *Hamlet*.

Krug and Ember talk about Hamlet and Ophelia: "Hamlet at Wittenberg, always late, missing G. Bruno's lectures . . ." (114). Bruno is the philosopher of the coincidence of contraries, who was burned to death at the stake — if not by the State, at least by a system that could allow no variety (in the form of heretics). Bruno was also a man who gave his faith to argument in words; his faith and his fate thus correspond to Hamlet's and Krug's. Nabokov gives us Hamlet as the indecisive poet who is unwilling or unable to act so long as he lacks the necessary evidence or the proper moment; he is always, therefore, on the horns of a dilemma. Krug is the indecisive philosopher who is unwilling to act because, though he knows men are irrational, he cannot believe in their irrationality. At one moment, Ember "might have embraced his fat friend [Krug] in silence (a miserable defeat in the case of philosophers and poets accustomed to believe that words are superior to deeds) . . ." (107). Words are superior — but only in value. Yet, paradoxically, Hamlet and Krug, and even Ember, are true individuals — that is, they are men of courage and strength.

The discussion of *Hamlet* is, then, an element in the satire about the political dream. The grotesque ideas of the stupid Professor Hamm in his "The Real Plot of *Hamlet*," which control Ember's production of the play in the new State Theater, are a revelation of Ekwilism: spiritual leveling on the one hand, racism on the other; and both the leveling and racism are intensely opposed to individualism. (Hamm and Durning-Lawrence, though opposed, are true brothers since they both deny Shakespeare in the name of political and economic classes.) We must finally allow the other meanings of "sinister" in the title *Bend Sinister;* although all things in the universe may be related, Nabokov does not believe that all things are of equal value. Both Paduk and Durning-Lawrence are sinister.

In the same way, the linguistic game that Krug and Ember play with names, their indulgence in that human and civililzed pleasure in words, is a spiritual activity which the Ekwilist mentality cannot tolerate or comprehend (unless we grant that Paduk's silly anagrams on Adam Krug's name, such as Gumakrad, Gurdamak, Dramaguk, can be called a pleasure in language). Nevertheless, Paduk misses the real significance of Krug's name: Adam is Hebrew for "the Man," the first man, the archetype of the individual. And Krug is Russian for "circle," "the circle in Krug, one Krug in another one" (39); and, therefore, he is the symbol of completeness as well as of contraries and complexity.

Ophelia also brings in things Russian, or at least Nabokov's joy in things Russian, as well as his joy in things sexual. But even the Russian, the sexual, and Ophelia are essentially elements in the serious game of words. Ember pursues the meaning and derivation of Ophelia's name. He, or rather Nabokov, again cribs enthusiastically from Shakespearean commentators such as John Ruskin and C. Elliot Browne. Nabokov, in his own text and by allusion, finds her name in Greek, Danish, Italian, and Latin — a name associated with serpents (with no Freudian meaning) and with amorous shepherds. She is "lithe, lithping, thin-lipped Ophelia, Amleth's wet dream, a mermaid of Lethe, a rare water serpent, *Russalka letheana* of science (to match your long purples)" (116). *Rusalka* is Russian for "mermaid," in particular a fresh-water mermaid with legs.[20] There is surely an allusion here to the mermaid of Pushkin's poem "Rusalka," a seductress who temps a lonely hermit into a lake and so to physical and spiritual death. Thus, both the mermaid and Ophelia (the creations of Shakespeare and Pushkin) are linked by allusion and description to the silly but destructive girl-child, Mariette, of Nabokov's novel. Mariette tempts Krug to a sexual death and hands him over to a physical death; and she is the youngest of three sisters, Mariette, Linda Bachofen, and Doktor von Wytwyl, all of whom help to wreck Krug's life, a kind of a diabolic Kore-Persephone-Hecate.

In this chapter Nabokov also makes most striking and pleasurable use of such connective devices as parallelisms, alliterations, metaphor, and even rhyme. He "quotes" Professor Hamm, whose style is a fog of clichés and blurred metaphors. Hamm is no Hamlet (let me laugh a little too, gentlemen, as Humbert Humbert says): "Some dark deed of violence . . . some masonic maneuver engendered by the Shylocks of high finance, has dispossessed" (110) Fortinbras' family of its right to the Danish throne; or "the poison poured into the sleeper's ear is a symbol of this subtle injection of lethal rumours . . ." (111). Once more we have, in Hamm's language, the idiom of the bureaucratic propagandist (state or private), a truly dead language; but this language is at least a delight in that it is a joke. Yet later, when Krug receives the various missives of the state, especially its newspapers, the gray pall is not funny but terrifying. (We should note that Nabokov points out, in his introduction to the *Time Reading Program* edition, that some of the language of Paduk's state comes directly from Russian sources, including the Russian constitution.)[21]

However, a phrase as wild as "lusty old King Hamlet smiting with a poleax the Polacks skidding and sprawling on the ice" (114 - 15), which is paraphrased Shakespeare-Krug and pure Nabokov, fits felicitously into its context; for the sound evokes the image. And when Ember's Hamlet says of Ophelia, "Quietly, with a kind of devilish daintiness she minced her dangerous course the way her father's ambition" (117) points, the line that elsewhere would be arch is, in context, both exact parody and significant statement.

We can add that the language of the country and the names of the characters are illustrations of this complex of associations. The language is a made-up one, just as is that of Zembla in *Pale Fire*. Its roots are Russian and Teutonic, although there are considerable patches of straight Russian, especially in the translations that Ember is making. However, the intent of the game is to connect Nabokov's "pasts" (*his* linguistic worlds) and, more seriously, to suggest that man's language creates, in major part, man's world. We may remark, too, that language is man's way of stopping (or passing) time.

The names serve not only as linkages but as humor (puns, even if erudite, give pleasure and connect). Krug is, to repeat, "circle." Paduk is nicknamed the Toad; his surname is almost "paddock," a toad. The word "paddock" certainly hints at something more threatening than does "toad"; in Shakespeare, it is almost always a symbol of evil. And the name of old Skotoma, the senile "philosopher" of Ekwilism, is a direct transliteration of the Modern Greek *skotoma*, "murder" or "killing." The comic-strip hero Etermon, who supplies a sartorial style and a manner of life for Paduk, is, as Nabokov indicates, Everyman; but there is a possible sarcasm here on *etymon*, the "true" or original meaning of a word, for Etermon is completely fake, both as an individual and as a symbol. Finally, we have the student Phokus, the nucleus of a resistance to Paduk, who appears in the novel only as a shape and a sound: Phokus is *fokus*, the Russian for "focus" as well as for "conjuring trick." Phokus is the novel's heart; but he is hidden, like those crown jewels in *Pale Fire*.

In Krug's dream in Chapter 5, we see most clearly this combination of real and unreal, of fiction and actuality, in the absurdity that is the art dream. "It bristled with with farcical anachronism . . ." (61). The dream is treated almost as a play, the play within the play. But "who is behind the timid producers?" And the dreamer, not Krug, answers, "A nameless, mysterious genius who took advantage of the dream to convey his own peculiar code message which has nothing," really, to do with "Krug's physical existence, but which links him somehow with an unfathomable mode of being . . . , a kind of transcendental madness which lurks behind the corner of consciousness . . . " (62), which links him, in fact, to Cincinnatus.

Yet the dream is also a flashback, a witty retelling of the story of old Skotoma. It also tells of Paduk senior and his padograph — a machine that reproduces handwriting, a machine, which, as an Ekwilist symbol, is taken to demonstrate "that a mechanical device can reproduce personality, and that Quality is merely the distributional aspect of Quantity" (68). The dream further tells of the founding by Paduk junior, the future dictator, of the Party of the Average Man, the schoolboy members of which are most unaverage since each is either mentally deficient or physically unfit — Nabokov's ironies are sometimes neither subtle nor pleasant. This part of Krug's dream is not a true dream sequence; it is Nabokov once more entering, slyly, as guide, since "a closer inspection (made when the dream-self is dead for the ten thousandth time and the day-self inherits for the ten thousandth time those dusty trifles . . .) reveals the presence of someone in the know. . . . and we start afresh now combining dim dreams with the scholarly precision of memory" (62 - 63). Here, in summary, is the process by which the artist works.

But for what purpose does he work? We must agree, finally, that

Bend Sinister makes the statement that there are kinds of lives and kinds of human activities — especially the activity that is art — which are of supreme value. And so we appropriately conclude this section with two quotations from Krug and one from William Butler Yeats that summarize Nabokov's themes in *Bend Sinister*. Krug, looking at notes for an essay that he "had never written and would never write because . . . he had forgotten its leading idea, its secret combination," thinks, "Lives that I envy: longevity, peaceful times, peaceful country, quiet fame, quiet satisfaction: Ivar Aasen, Norwegian philologist, 1813 - 1896, who invented a language. Down here we have too much of *homo civis* and too little of *sapiens*" (157). The *homo sapiens* includes the kind of man who invents languages (and Aasen really existed), since language is humankind's greatest glory. *Sapiens* also includes the writer, for writing comes from language. Language and art are the essences of life, life which Krug thinks of as "consciousness, which is the only real thing in the world and the greatest mystery of all" (186). And yet, as Yeats said, "in dreams begins responsibility." If Nabokov's novel is a dream, it is one that says that we have responsibilities for other human beings.

CHAPTER 7

The American Novels

I Lolita

What is the evil deed I have committed?
Seducer, criminal — is this the word
for me who set the entire world a-dreaming
of my poor little girl?

THESE lines, written first in Russian in 1959, are the opening stanza of Nabokov's wry response to the moralist critics of *Lolita*,[1] his third novel in English; his first American one in subject matter and in certain attitudes; his only English novel that he has valued enough to translate into Russian (1967); and by far his most famous novel — the one in which he gave English a new meaning to an old word, "nymphet." According to many but perhaps less moral critics, *Lolita* is his finest novel; and it is the one for which he feels "the most affection."[2] It is certainly the novel in which his major characters, interesting and usually sympathetic, are most directly related to his concerns with art itself.

Nabokov admits that "It was my most difficult book — the book that treated of the theme which was so distant, so remote, from my own emotional life that it gave me a special pleasure to use my combinational talent to make it real."[3] The combinations of themes, structures, images, ideas, and characters are many; and the stanza I have quoted does not contain the essential statement of the poem and one of the essential statements of the novel; for, Nabokov adds, "at the last indention/ . . ./ a Russian branch's shadow shall be playing/ upon the marble of my hand."[4] The novel does treat a theme utterly remote from Nabokov's own emotional life if we mean that of Humbert Humbert's obsession; but Nabokov is, nevertheless, contained within the novel. The novel is also a Russian novel, and so

115

his own representation is there, not just as Vivian Darkbloom, who is
the collaborator with Clare Quilty on the play, *The Lady who Loved
Lightning*,[5] and who has just completed a biography called "My
Cue." This title makes certain that the reader recognizes that the
character, Quilty, belongs not only to Vivian Darkbloom but to
"her" anagrammatic creator. Although we must accept Nabokov's
disclaimers — Lolita is not his Colette, for example; and his
childhood experience with her is not Humbert Humbert's with Annabel Leigh — he has again used but transcended his own experience by using his imagination and by making it into art.

Experience transcended makes the novel not only American but
Nabokovian American. "It had taken me some forty years to invent
Russia and Western Europe, and now I was faced by the task of inventing America" (314), he says of his first steps toward the novel.
Written largely in the summers that he and his wife spent in the
American West on butterfly-hunting trips, the description of the
landscape of Humbert Humbert's and Lolita's nightmare journey is
quintessentially American; but the landscape has been made new by
a mind which could really see our land and our experience. But,
when *Lolita* was finished, Nabokov could find no American
publisher; and he turned in some ignorance, he claims, to Maurice
Girodias' Olympia Press in Paris — one best known for its por-
nography. The book was published in 1955 in two green, paper-
covered volumes, a book about America that could not, apparently,
be published in the States because it was too "perverse." *Lolita's*
perversity, not its picture of America or its brilliance, made it a best
seller in America when it was finally published in the States in 1958:
"Hurricane/Lolita swept from Florida to Maine," John Shade wrote
in *Pale Fire*. As a result of the novel's sales, Nabokov was freed from
teaching, which he enjoyed but which took time from his art; and
not just his artistic conscience lies behind his admission that he
shudders "retrospectively when I recall that there was a moment, in
1950, and again in 1951, when I was on the point of burning
Humbert Humbert's little black diary."[6]

The history of the novel's composition, if Nabokov's afterword,
"On a Book Entitled *Lolita*," is to be believed, contains the controlling image, as we shall see, of the novel: "The first little throb of
Lolita went through me late in 1939 or early in 1940, in
Paris, . . . the initial shiver of inspiration was somehow prompted by
a newspaper story about an ape in the Jardin des Plantes, who, after
months of coaxing by a scientist, produced the first drawing ever

charcoaled by an animal: this sketch showed the bars of the poor creature's cage" (313). The initial result of Nabokov's inspiration was the short story "Volshebnik" ("The Magician"), written in Russian, which was never published.[7] The hero, the magician (one more magician), was "a Central European, the anonymous nymphet was French, and the loci were Paris and Provence." The hero marries the little girl's mother, who providentially dies; and the man, after "a thwarted attempt to take advantage of the orphan in a hotel room" (314), throws himself under a truck and is killed. This basic plot and image were far from the complexity and the Americanness of *Lolita*.

A more direct impulse for the novel's plot is found in Nabokov's *The Gift* in a story related by the disgusting and crude stepfather of Zina Mertz, Boris Ivanovich Shchyogolev, who tells Fyodor that he too has thought of being a writer since he has a tale "from real life." Shchyogolev's own story is disguised slightly, for the nonartist always believes that simple transcription from life makes art. Shchyogolev suggests that he married Zina's mother because he had an itch for her daughter: "Here you can go on indefinitely — the temptation, the eternal torment. . . . And the upshot — a miscalculation. . . . D'you feel here a kind of Dostoevskian tragedy?"[8]

Transposed to America, Nabokov's subjects came together — plot, characters, metaphor, loci, and moral — and so his worlds came together too. The plot, as Nabokov finally works it out, is once again simple; it is always the telling that makes the "combinational delight." In brief, *Lolita* relates the story of Humbert Humbert's obsessive love for Dolores Haze, a love that directly and indirectly leads to their deaths. The chronology is not the structure, but the chronology is the "story." Humbert Humbert was born in Paris in 1910; his father was "a salad of racial genes"; and his mother, an Englishwoman (shades of *Sebastian Knight*), was killed by lightning when Humbert was an infant (lightning is a significant image in the novel). Humbert is reared, therefore, by his mother's sister, whose husband is in America.

At thirteen, Humbert met Annabel Leigh, daughter of a Mrs. Leigh who was "born Vanessa van Ness"; and in these names Nabokov alludes not only to Edgar Allen Poe's "Annabel Lee" and, through Poe's poem, to Poe's child wife, Virginia Clemm but also to Jonathan Swift's Vanessa, Esther Vanhomrigh. The references are to the stories of young girls who were involved with older men. But Nabokov also alludes to the *Vanessa atalanta*, the Red Admirable (Admiral) butterfly, whose names, by the way, magically appear in

Jonathan Swift's "Cadenus and Vanessa." The worlds of English and American literature and of lepidoptery reinforce, therefore, the themes of the novel.

Humbert's and Annabel's adolescent love affair is never, although almost, consummated; but, after his loss of her, Humbert has a fixation for a certain type of not-quite-pubescent girl child as a sexual object. He even invents the word "nymphet," an entomologist's word, for his preferred little girl. This idea, which is incarnated in Lolita Haze, ruins his life; but, paradoxically, it is only through knowing the actual girl that he grows out of his sickness.

After Humbert's unsuccessful marriage to a Polish woman, whom he married because of her childlikeness, which is childishness, he arrives in America, for he has inherited his uncle's perfume business. He can never be a successful businessman since his life is not only literarily but sexually obsessed. His obsession causes him to break down; he is hospitalized and then released; he goes to the Arctic on a farcical expedition; and, returned, he spends a summer in the New England town of Ramsdale. There he rents a room at 342 Lawn Street with a Mrs. Charlotte Haze (342, a number that is repeated again and again in the novel in different contexts, is the novel's connecting number). Humbert takes the room because he has caught a glimpse of the widowed Mrs. Haze's pre-adolescent daughter, Dolores or Lolita. Humbert falls in love: "It was love at first sight, at last sight, at ever and ever sight" (272).

Humbert Humbert, F. W. Dupee notes, "is an ironic portrait of the visiting European, and the Hazes help to complete the likeness. He is to them somehow the prince of a lost realm . . . [and] he seems to have the superior sexual acumen and appeal so often assumed by Europeans and connived at by Americans. . . ."[9] Humbert Humbert, fatally attractive, fascinates his American nymphet's mother; and, to be near the nymphet, he marries the woman. But unfortunately Humbert keeps a diary, and Charlotte Haze finds it. Dashing across the street to mail the leters that will reveal him to the world, she is struck by a car and killed — an ironic reversal of the death of the man in "The Magician." After his wife's death Humbert, in a sense, kidnaps Lolita who has been at camp and who does not know her mother is dead until after she and Humbert have spent their first night together in The Enchanted Hunters inn. Despite his elaborate plans, he does not seduce her but she him — one more irony of reversal, for Lolita is not an innocent in the sexual sense. Nevertheless, she is emotionally and morally innocent in the classic American tradition of innocence of Huckleberry Finn.

After this episode, the novel neatly divides into two sections. The second half covers their love affair, if it can be so called. They begin their incredible journey across America, seeing all its tourist sights and hundreds of its motels. Nabokov presents America as experienced by the traveler but by a traveler who lives it all, not just the surface. This trip is the death, however, of any possible love that Lolita could have had for Humbert; for the first night is the only night that she is willingly, happily, his. After it, she is his prisoner; for he convinces her, in order to hold her, that, if she ever reveals what they have done, she will be placed in some dreadful public institution which would be even worse than the life he has given her.

At the end of their first year, Humbert brings her back to the East and puts her in an excruciatingly progressive girls' school. He hopes in his way to establish a "family," but the result can only be a bitter parody of the family. Lolita almost fits into the school and so into a more conventional and happy life. She takes part in a play, *The Enchanted Hunters* — the connection with The Enchanted Hunters inn seems a joke connection, but it is only later that we learn that the man who will take Lolita away from Humbert Humbert is the writer of the play — and was at the inn on the night that Lolita and Humbert Humbert were there. Humbert suspects that she has found a new lover, takes her out of the school, and begins again an insane odyssey. They are now always going westward, the American direction. This time, however, Lolita chooses their route, and she does so in order that she may escape. She has found her "rescuer," but, in the moral world of the novel, he is to be even worse than Humbert Humbert.

Humbert at last notices that he and Lolita are being followed by a red "Aztec" convertible and that the man driving it bears a resemblance to his own uncle, Gustave Trapp. And the man and Humbert will, indeed, be relatives, if not by blood. The man even precedes Humbert, at least in a sense; in the town of "Wace, Continental Divide" (212), Humbert and Lolita see a play, written by Vivian Darkbloom and Clare Quilty, in which the rainbow girls are drawn from *Finnegans Wake* and in which a "father" desires his own daughter. The fact that one of the writers is Lolita's new lover becomes clear only later to Humbert Humbert.

At last, in the town of Elphinstone, Lolita flees. The remainder of the novel is about Humbert Humbert's search for her and the man with whom she ran away. When Humbert doubles back, examining registers of "342 hotels, motels and tourist homes," he discovers only that he and the man he seeks are oddly alike: "He mimed and mocked me. His allusions were definitely highbrow. He was well-read. He knew French. He was versed in logodaedaly and logomancy. He was an amateur of sex lore. He had a feminine handwriting. . . . His main trait was his passion for tantilization. Goodness, what a tease the poor fellow was! He challenged my scholarship" (251 - 52).

When Humbert meets Rita, a rather pathetic, childlike woman, her childlikeness attracts him; but he lives with her almost as though they were both mature. Although he himself has begun to grow up, he cannot forget either Lolita or the man who took her from him; his destiny must be fulfilled. Three years later, when he receives a letter from Lolita, she addresses him as "Dear Dad," a pathetic touch; and, after announcing that she is married and pregnant, she asks him for money. Humbert thinks that the man she married, Richard Schiller, is his enemy and prepares to kill him; but Schiller turns out to be a young and innocent veteran. Lolita tells Humbert the name of her lover — one given to the reader earlier. He is the playwright whose picture, an advertisement, was affixed to the wall of Lolita's room when her mother was still alive; he is supposedly physically similar to Humbert; he is the man who drove the "formidable convertible, resplendent, rubious" (119) of Humbert's and Lolita's first night at The Enchanted Hunters; and he is the man who is Humbert's double and the creature of their common creator. In short, he is Clare Quilty, who collaborated with Nabokov (that is, Vivian Darkbloom) on so many works.

When Humbert asks Lolita to return to him, she responds that she cannot: "I would sooner go back to Cue," to Quilty. "She groped for words. I supplied them mentally ('*He* broke my heart. *You* merely broke my life')" (281). And so Humbert Humbert sets off to kill the man who has deprived him of his only love. In a terrible and perversely funny scene, which makes the event more terrible, Humbert does kill him. Then he drives away; and, "since I had disregarded all laws of humanity, I might as well disregard the rules of traffic" (308). This gallows humor is the whole book's tone, for the serious and the comic combine. But the novel remains, in its own terms, yet to be written: Humbert drives off the road, the police arrive, and the story ends. He spends his last days writing his confession; but both he and Lolita must be dead before his book is published.

Of course, the story is not the meaning of the novel; it is hardly even its message. "*Lolita*," as Page Stegner indicates, "is a book that goes in many directions and works on its reader in many ways. . . .

[It is] comic, perverse, tragic, and grotesque," and, certainly, each of these things must be examined "separately, [although] they merge to produce a total artistic effect. . . ."[10] As for Nabokov, he, as usual, is both helpful and misleading. He insists, for instance, that "*Lolita* has no moral in tow" (316); and, in response to an interviewer's remark that "many critics have called the book a masterful satiric social commentary on America," he has asserted that he had "neither the intent nor the temperament of a moral or social satirist. . . . But I am annoyed when the glad news is spread that I am ridiculing America."[11] This last comment is, in particular, his reaction to certain anti-American French critics who hailed *Lolita* as an attack on America — critics whose attitudes toward a novel of this kind are so automatic as to be comic in themselves.

But Nabokov has also said that "an American critic [John Hollander] suggested that *Lolita* was the record of my love affair with the romantic novel. The substitution 'English language' for 'romantic novel' would make this elegant formula more correct" (318). We cannot ignore this statement: the book is not only about America but about language, English and American; for it is filled with the pleasure of language. But to leave the meaning of *Lolita* at that is to make its intent a bit inhuman, for the book's great success is in its living people and, in respect of Nabokov, in its moral. We must return for clarification to Nabokov's story of the ape, as well as to the story of Shchyogolev; for, behind these odd sources, lie intense human emotions. As I have suggested, the controlling image of *Lolita* is the one in the ape's story: the animal's "sketch showed the bars of the poor creature's cage" (313). Andrew Field argues cogently that the "image of the zoo and the cage, both figurative and real," are recurrent and significant images in Nabokov's work since he "understands the cage . . . as the dual metaphor of artistic form and human fate."[12] The plot of *Lolita* is the perversely successful attempt to escape from the cage: both Lolita, that lost child, and Humbert Humbert, that great sinner, are in cages; and, if they escape, they do so only through death: Lolita in that remote Northwest town of Gray Star — a fitting name for "the capital town of the book" (318) — and Humbert in his jail cell.

For Humbert Humbert is not utterly lost, despite sharing a moral perverseness with Shchyogolev and with the unspeakable Hermann of Nabokov's novel *Despair*. Unhappily, Humbert's own growth necessitates the use of Lolita, and herein lies the tragedy. "The final section of the novel," Page Stegner says, "seems to be a parody of

. . . redemption and purification through the destruction of the symbolic self (pervert Humbert slaughtering pervert Quilty)."[13] I agree
that parody is an essential element of the novel; but the "parody" is
in this instance a sign of morality.

The book is being written during some fifty-six prison days from
Humbert's hindsight, but we see and overhear his moral growth during his years with Lolita. He can, with absurdly self-serving
arguments, define the nymphet and then argue that nobody was up-
set that Dante "fell madly in love with his Beatrice when she was
nine" (21); he fails to admit that Dante was the same age as Beatrice
and that Humbert himself was twenty-five years older. But he can
also, with a beginning insight, perceive — as Lolita did the first
night after she had discovered that her mother was dead and "came
sobbing into [my bed]" — that "she had absolutely nowhere else to
go" (144). His statement is a cry of anguish and guilt. And he gets a
glimpse into what he has done to Lolita in his recollection of a moment when "fat Avis" Byrd held on to her father and he to her with
love, not lust; and "I saw Lolita's smile lose all its light."

At last, Humbert achieves this insight into himself as well as into
Lolita: "It had become gradually clear to my conventional Lolita
during our singular and bestial cohabitation that even the most miserable of family lives was better than the parody of incest, which, in
the long run, was the best I could offer the waif" (289). If Lolita is
conventional, so, in the end, is Humbert Humbert; but this conven-
tionality consists of recognizing that others have a right to their own
lives and that one does not use others. And the final moral is contained in Humbert's words on the last pages of the novel: he has told
the whole story, but he now recalls a day not long after Lolita had
run away when he, high in the western mountains, has listened to

a melodious unity of sounds rising like vapor from a small mining town that
lay at my feet, in a fold of the valley. . . . And soon I realized that all these
sounds were of one nature, that no other sounds but these came from the
streets of the transparent town. . . . What I heard was but the melody of
children at play, nothing but that. . . . and then I knew that the hopelessly
poignant thing was not Lolita's absence from my side, but the absence of her
voice from that concord (309 - 10).

What he has deprived her of is her childhood — and so, in a manner,
her life; for we never recover a lost childhood. The book celebrates
and regrets all lost childhoods, as well as all lost time.

Nevertheless, the novel's meaning cannot be encompassed entirely by positive moral generalizations. The book is not didactic; and it is not a satire upon America. To Nabokov, "Satire is a lesson, parody is a game",[14] but, though he rejects lessons, he is always willing to play a game. Yet games are more than mere entertainment; the games the novelist plays involve the whole human being: *homo ludens* is *homo sapiens*. *Lolita*, therefore, is a parody, as Appel and many others argue; and it is a parody of infinite complexity. As I have remarked before, parody encloses, contains, and shares with what it is mocking; and *Lolita* is a parody of the biography, of the picaresque form, and of the whole mythic quest.

This larger quest, of course, contains within itself smaller quests, smaller parodies: the journey that Humbert Humbert takes in pursuit of the man who has stolen Lolita is a version of the detective's quest, and so we have one more distant analogy with Poe, who invented the detective story for Americans. But, more to the parodic point, there are analogies, not too distant, to the Alice stories, and to Charles Lutwidge Dodgson, alias Lewis Carroll, who dearly loved to photograph young girls, especially in the nude, but who thought his interest absolutely innocent. Carroll, Nabokov admits, "has a pathetic affinity with H. H. . . . ,"[15] but his references to Carroll are much more significant in *Pale Fire* than in *Lolita*.

But, once more, even the apparently strictly literary parodies relate to the people, to the human meaning, of the novel. As an example, among the several parodies of poems which Humbert Humbert recites to Quilty there is that mad farrago which is, we recognize, a take-off on T. S. Eliot's "Ash Wednesday"; but Eliot's poem is also a type of parody, for it is based on Guido Cavalcanti's "Perch' io non spero di tornar," which is, at the last, a lament for a lost beloved.

If Nabokov's mindless Shchyogolev gives the basic plot of *Lolita* and adds, "D'you feel here a kind of Dostoevskian tragedy?", we can, in regard to *Lolita*, answer yes. Although Nabokov does not like Dostoevsky, he nevertheless uses him; for Svidrigaylov commits suicide in *Crime and Punishment* because he has raped and murdered a small girl. Or, to repeat, what Nabokov attacks in *Lolita* is human insensitivity, the failure of one human being to allow another to live fully.

But the novel is more than a moral message or a statement on America. It is also a form; it has a structure — a spiral that contains within itself its own time, escaping time. And so we cannot ignore an addition that has become a real part of the novel — Nabokov's own

afterword which was written after the novel itself was first published
and which comments from outside the novel's time. In this addition,
Nabokov speaks of the artistic problem of what author and work are
— how, in brief, time becomes one: "After doing my impersonation
of suave John Ray, the character in *Lolita* who pens the Foreword,
any comments coming straight from me may strike one — may strike
me, in fact — as an impersonation of Vladimir Nabokov talking
about his own book" (313). Of course, the work is about art and artist: Humbert Humbert is his author — but who is impersonating
whom is difficult to determine. The final "message" of the novel,
not the moral one, is contained in the last words that Humbert
Humbert writes. These words, addressed to his beloved Lolita who
will never read them, praises art for creating people and for overcoming time: "one wanted H. H. to exist at least a couple of months
longer, so as to have him make you live in the minds of later
generations. I am thinking of aurochs and angels, the secret of
durable pigments, prophetic sonnets, the refuge of art. And this is
the only immortality you and I may share, my Lolita" (311).

II   Pnin

Nabokov's thirteenth novel and his fourth novel in English, *Pnin*,
was published in the United States in 1957; although it was written
after *Lolita*, it preceded American publication of the latter by a year.
Four of the seven chapters of the novel were printed first in *The
New Yorker* before the whole was published as a book. Asked if he
had conceived of the novel as a whole, Nabokov answered that "the
design of *Pnin* was complete in my mind when I composed the first
chapter which, I believe, in this case was actually the first of the
seven I physically set down."[16] This reference to his writing habits
indicates that, after a work has been planned in his mind, Nabokov
works from almost any place toward the whole. It also indicates that
the structure and the meanings of his novels are seldom the chance
inspiration of the moment of writing. However, *Pnin* does seem to
lack structure; it does seem a series of short stories. But the novel has
as its central character the most charming of Nabokov's heroes and
is, as a consequence, one of his most delightful and one of his best
novels.

Until *Pale Fire*, *Pnin* was the only novel that reflected Nabokov's
own academic teaching experience; in this respect, we should note
Alfred Appel's implication when he points out that *Pnin* is the only
novel in which Nabokov ever felt it necessary to include the standard

statement (unless we admit the joke disclaimer of *Ada*) that "All the characters in this book are fictitious, and any resemblance to actual persons, living or dead, is purely coincidental."[17] The novel is not only a structure, but it is about the external world. In brief, the novel is a satire, albeit a gentle one. As Ambrose Gordon, Jr. says, this satire on the academy "is no more this novel's chief concern than was satire of motels the chief concern of *Lolita*."[18]

The story or rather the stories told in *Pnin* are simple, but they all relate to one another so that the structure is more precise than it seems. Structurally, the novel is another spiral, the means by which it contains itself as well as the story or stories. The "story's" time, in the sense of the time covered in its "present," includes the period from 1950 to February 15, 1955; but, since the actual time covered in its flashbacks is from 1911 to February 15, 1955, the structure both denies and asserts time. What the story tells is the life of Timofey Pnin, who was born into a comfortable family life in Russia; was exiled by the Revolution; lived a life of intellectual endeavor among the Russian émigrés of Western Europe; fell in love with a woman named Liza Bogolepov who did not love him but who used him; married her; was abandoned and divorced by her; came to America and taught — teaches, in the novel's present — Russian at Waindell College; entertains various American colleagues and is visited by Liza and by her son from her husband after Pnin; and, as the book closes, departs from Waindell for some unknown place.

But such a summary gives us no sense of the book's meanings nor of its delights, for it is a very delightful book. The dust jacket of the first edition of the novel give us an insight into both meaning and delight; it contains a picture of Timofey Pavlovich Pnin himself, "ideally bald, . . . cleanshaven, . . . with that great brown dome of his, tortoise-shell glasses (masking an infantile absence of eyebrows), apish upper lip, thick neck, and strongman torso" — and we can imagine the rest, the "pair of spindly legs . . . and frail-looking, almost feminine feet."[19] In Pnin's left hand is a book entitled, in Cyrillic (Russian) letters, PNIN [by] V. Nabokov. Although the illustration does not tell us that Pnin is also a foreigner; an outsider; a mere untenured professor of Russian at Waindell College; a man already in his fifties; and one who is almost a *schlemihl*, the unlucky, foolish victim, although not the cliché the *schlemihl* is, it gives us a brilliant insight. The picture of Pnin holding a book entitled *Pnin* suggests the fact that the novel is about the production of a work of art as well as about the character of Pnin. In the novel, Pnin is a lonely, learned, comic, fascinating, and absurd émigré Russian lost in American academia — but he does not know that he is lost, for he has almost always, at least within himself, his dignity. More generally, as Gordon argues, the novel is a picture of the "figure of the Banished Man" in "its dual components of the [sad] Exile and the [funny] Alien";[20] however, the novel contains more humor than Gordon suggests.

And this novel repeats, therefore, the Nabokov themes of loss and yet of dignity. For Pnin, a man whose very existence depends upon language, is in a world where his own language, Russian, does not help him organize experience. He should be pitiful, but Nabokov does not let him be pitiful, and Pnin will not let himself be that. If, as R. H. W. Dillard argues, Pnin, who is different from most of Nabokov's heroes concerned with language, "is neither the artist-hero nor the mad artist failure,"[21] we must respond that he is in his own way an artist. As Andrew Field suggests, *Pnin* is a novel whose "narrative movement . . . is the flight of a character from his author";[22] nevertheless the character frees himself and so creates himself. The "artist" in this novel is the narrator, the "I" who tells the story; and, if there is a symbiotic relationship between him and Pnin, there is also a distance, just as there is a distance between Pnin and Nabokov. Pnin is, paradoxically, the most assertive of Nabokov's characters; and, because he is, he can only be hugely comic.

The story is told by an "I" who is both omnisicient teller and disembodied character; for the narrator has his effect upon the action, although he himself does not really appear until the last chapter and although the reader does not really see him even then. The narrator is never directly named, although a friend of Pnin's remarks at one moment that a certain Vladimir Vladimirovich would know the names of certain blue butterflies (128) — it is delightfully significant that Pnin disparages this Vladimir Vladimirovich — and the narrator later speaks of his own interest in butterfly hunting (177). The narrator is, in short, Nabokov; although the narrator is not the actual Nabokov who wrote the book, he is that character, the author who tells the story, whom Nabokov sometimes impersonates.

Andrew Field, speaking of this novel, suggests that there are two techniques by which the narrator can observe without himself becoming a central figure: first, "by means of documents and personal accounts"; second, "by means of the narrator who is merely a pretext on the part of the author and is only remembered from time to time. . . ." *Pnin*, he says, follows the first method,[23] but it does so with a change since the knowledge that "I" has of certain moments in Pnin's life could only be obtained by an act of the imagination. The narrator is not forgotten by the author; the narrator is, rather, the author; and the narrator-author's act of recreating Pnin's life invites us to observe the imagination as it works. The novel is a process for the author and for the reader.

In the final chapter, we are only in the "I's" mind; for Pnin has made his own self-assertion and has moved away, not only from the narrator-author but from Nabokov. However, during the time of the novel, as Field argues, the narrator is an aggressive intruder into Pnin's life. And if Pnin escapes in the end, fleeing Waindell to avoid coming into contact with the narrator, he does not really escape Nabokov; for Pnin, or at least his namesake, has another job and a new life in *Pale Fire* in which "a bald-headed suntanned professor in a Hawaiian shirt [sits] . . . reading . . . a Russian book." He is the "Head of the bloated Russian Department" and a "regular martinet in regard to his underlings" at Wordsmith University.[24]

Although most of *Pnin* is about comic Pnin at Waindell, the past, given in bits, endows comic Pnin with seriousness. Characteristically for Nabokov, the first encounter between the narrator and Pnin is not reported until the last chapter. The encounter occurred soon after the narrator's twelfth birthday, on a spring day in 1911. The narrator is exactly the same age as Nabokov — and both lived in a "rosy-stone house in the Morskaya" Street in St. Petersburg. Getting something in his eye, the narrator goes to Dr. Pavel Pnin, a noted ophthalmologist; and there he is introduced to the doctor's thirteen-year-old son. This encounter with Pnin is the event; and its meaning is indicated in the narrator's remarks about "the offending black atom" that was removed from his eye: "I wonder where that speck is now? The dull, mad fact is that it *does* exist somewhere" (175 - 76). And indeed it does, as all the past continues to exist, even if transformed, even if distorted and made new by memory.

For the next memory that the "I" has of himself and of Pnin is of the summer of 1916 when Pnin and another young man came to ask the narrator's grandaunt if they could use a barn of hers for the production of a play in which they will both act. The narrator attends the performance; "next to me sat the steward of my aunt's estate, Robert Karlovich Horn" (178), nearly the name that the creative reader noted in the first section of the book as that of a young American twenty-four years later. The past is in the present, but the present precedes the past in the art work. But the event is not

what is important: the importance is that, when the narrator and
Pnin meet around 1925, Pnin denies the particulars of their
meetings; and the narrator comments that, "noticing how reluctant
he was to recognize his own past, I switched to another, less personal
topic" (180). But the question of what is true has been answered by
the fact that it is the "author's" recreation of the past in his imagination that we are given and which we accept. Once more, "Imagination is a form of memory."[25]

At this same evening in 1925, the narrator meets the young
medical student, Liza Bogolepov, who believes herself a poet; and
she ties the narrator's and Pnin's lives almost indissolubly together.
Almost immediately the narrator and Liza have an affair; and Pnin is
already, or soon to be, in love with her, a love from which he never
recovers. However, the narrator soon tires of Liza; her poetry, filled
with feeling and artistically poor, offends his artistic conscience.
Poor Pnin writes Liza a letter of proposal, saying that he is not
"handsome, . . . not interesting, . . . not talented, . . . not even rich."
He adds with his own innocent honesty a criticism of her rather absurd ideas about psychology; Pnin still keeps, even if unwittingly, his
integrity which in the end is his dignity. When Liza departs after
visiting him at Waindell, he does, however, cry to Joan Clements,
one of his few friends, that "I haf nofing left, nofing, nofing!" (61)
and becomes a comic, a pitiful figure. But he recovers,
magnificently, always.

Liza leaves Pnin in 1938 for the obnoxious, "psychoasinine" (50)
Eric Wind, "a man who understood her 'organic ego' "! (46). But just
as Pnin prepares, in Nabokov's 1940, to sail for the United States,
Liza, pregnant, returns to him and announces that she will stay with
him forever. Pnin arranges everything, getting her visa and passage
on the ship. But her return is a trick; Wind is on the ship too, and
they have used Pnin to get Liza to America. Wind offers, however, to
pay half of Liza's passage. "Ach nein, nein, nein," Pnin cries in comic, sad Russian-German. "Let us finish this nightmare conversation
(diese koschmarische Sprache)" (49). "Koschmarische" is not German but Russian; derived from French, it is Russian for "nightmare."

Pnin is the eternal victim, and even language victimizes him, for it
does not obey him. As Irwin Weil remarks, Pnin's whole American
experience shows "the Russian sensibility confronting the American
[one may substitute 'non-Russian'] language," as for instance in the
statement of "Pnin's regret that English quotations from

Shakespeare can never match the richness and power of the Russian originals in his memory from childhood."[26]

In America, Pnin is the comic, blundering Alien; but, because he has kept Russia with him, he does not perceive this fact. Language, with its treacheries and its beauties, is at the very center of the novel as part of the point of view and as the strategy of the narrator. The narrator reports what he has been told, but he reshapes it; and Pnin is thus made both tragic and comic at the same moment. After that visit by his adored and insensitive Liza, he stumbles around, looking for whiskey and soda; Joan Clements, coming in, asks him what he is doing. " 'I search, John, for the viscous and sawdust,' he said tragically" (59). We must and can laugh at Pnin here; for, if the episode were presented without humor, it would not express sentiment or feeling, but treacly sentimentality.

These stories of Pnin's early life are, as I have noted, contained within the present; and the present makes up the body of the novel; the present contains the past: story, character, episodes, language, are all one. The first episode tells of Pnin's comic mishaps on his journey from Waindell to Cremona where he is to give a lecture on "Are the Russian People Communist?"; the novel ends with Jack Cockerell, head of the English department at Waindell College, about to give an imitation of Pnin who is about to give the wrong lecture at the Cremona Women's Club. The novel has gone, not full circle, but full spiral; for the same event, Pnin's lecture, is to be repeated but not in the same form.

Particular images that reinforce this shape, this spiral, make the world one. As Pnin sits, waiting to be introduced for his lecture, he has an odd vision, the result of the small heart attack he has suffered earlier in the day, in which he sees the women in the hall transformed into people from his own past, from a moment in 1912; the "vision" includes his own father whom we see in greater detail in the last chapter. Earlier there has been Bob Horn, who is to be transmuted to, or from, Robert Karlovich Horn. And, later, the painter Lake conceives of the solar spectrum not as a circle which starts with red on one end and goes through violet on the other to return to red, but as a spiral that goes beyond violet to a "lavender gray" and then into "Cinderella" colors beyond the range of "human perception."

Lake's idea is the idea and the image of the novel. For, since the artistic process is in part a search for and creation of the correspondences that give structure, as I have argued in the first chapter of this book, then each novel must reflect all possible correspondences. Lake teaches, for instance, that a work of art can and must be made a part of the natural world. A motor car as a subject for a painting becomes a part of nature by having "the scenery penetrate the automobile. . . . This mimetic and integrative process Lake called the necessary 'naturalization' of man-made things" (96 - 97).

Within the work, certain dates, such as February 15, are means to this process. But the correspondences reach out to all of Nabokov's works. Pnin lives in the house that he purchases at 999 Todd Road; John Shade's "Pale Fire," in the novel of the same name, has 999 lines (or maybe 1000, if one repeats the first line at the end, making yet another spiral). Moreover, Shade says in a minor poem, "The Nature of Electricity," that lamps, those burning lights, may house souls and that "maybe/[streetlamp] Number nine-hundred-ninety-nine/. . ./. . . is an old friend of mine."[27] He is indeed. There is a painter, Lang, in *Pnin*, whose Waindell College mural mixes historical figures with faculty members; and the painter Lang in *Pale Fire* paints the portrait of John Shade's wife.

But there is one more connection that must be taken into consideration since it gives us Pnin's values as well as Nabokov's. In chapter 4, Pnin is visited by the fourteen-year-old, "tall, tall, tall" Victor Wind, Liza and Eric's son. Pnin loves Victor; Victor likes Pnin; Victor is the son that Pnin never had. Victor is a painter, and his "eye was his supreme organ" (94). Nabokov has said that he himself was born to be a painter, and the eye is concerned with the exact appearances that make the work of art. However, the major significance is that the chapter begins with Victor's continuing daydream of himself as the son of a king of a vaguely Balkan country — a standard adolescent daydream, that is more meaningful to Victor because his parents pay so little attention to him. The king is about to be forced into exile by a revolution: there is a "crucial flight episode when the King alone — *solus rex* (as chess problem makers term royal solitude) — paced a beach on the Bohemian Sea, at Tempest Point, where Percival Blake, a cheerful American adventurer had promised to meet him with a powerful motorboat" (86).

The immediate connections are with Nabokov's unfinished Russian novel "Solus Rex," two parts of which were published in 1940 and 1942, which also concerns the theme of exile and with the novel *Pale Fire* in which almost the same story is told about how Charles the Beloved, Charles Kinbote, escapes from his distant northern kingdom, Zembla. And Nabokov writes in the English poem, "An Evening of Russian Poetry," which I have already cited:

> Beyond the seas where I have lost a sceptre,
> I hear the neighing of my dappled nouns,
> Soft participles coming down the steps, . . .

Nabokov, Pnin, Charles Kinbote are all exiles; and, in essence, they are in exile from that home which is language. The fourth chapter in *Pnin* closes with Pnin's dream, which is by artistic sleight of hand a continuation of Victor's, of his "son's": "Pnin saw himself fantastically cloaked, fleeing through great pools of ink under a cloud-barred moon from a chimerical palace, and then pacing a desolate strand with his dead friend Ilya Isidorovich Polyanski as they waited for some mysterious deliverance to arrive in a throbbing boat from beyond the hopeless sea." But the night wears on and "On the sandy beach where Pnin was still pacing (his worried friend had gone home for a map), there appeared before him a set of approaching footprints, and he awoke with a gasp. His back hurt" (109-10).

Poor Pnin, like Charles Kinbote, will remain forever in exile. But his exile is, like Lolita's, magnificent; for he will "live in the minds of later generations" in short, in "the refuge of art." But Pnin is not just in art; he makes it. In *Bend Sinister*, Krug presents the idea of a certain "director" for a new filming of *Hamlet* that will include a scene of Ophelia in the water surrounded by flowers and thereby is associated with phallic orchises and phallic snakes. Pnin, reading in a book about Russian myths, is fascinated by a passage about peasant maidens making wreaths of buttercups and frog orchises which, on Whitsunday, are "shaken down into the river, where, unwinding, they floated like so many serpents while the maidens floated and chanted among them" (77). Because the two novels are connected, the Nabokovian universe expands and Nabokov's values are reinforced. For Pnin, the description of the ancient custom is a reminder of Russian culture and so of his own life; for the reader, the associations remind us that literature preserves and is our culture, our best values.

CHAPTER 8

The Artist of Two Worlds

I   Pale Fire

L OLITA was a success, both artistic and financial; and *Pale Fire*,[1] the novel that followed in terms of publication in the United States, was also a best seller — for a short while. But, since this work was an obscure, exasperating book, most readers found that both in sex and in sense it failed to measure up to their expectations. Even the literati were divided; to some, such as Mary McCarthy, the novel was a work of genius; according to others, it was a hoax or an ambitious failure. Miss McCarthy was right, for *Pale Fire* is a significant work. But it is a Chinese box within a Chinese box within. The novel is, first, the poem "Pale Fire"; written in couplets, the poem has nine hundred and ninety-nine lines plus one, for the first line, or at least the rhyme of the first one, is to be repeated as the one thousandth. Divided into four cantos, the poem was composed by John Francis Shade (born July 5, 1898; died July 21, 1959) during the last twenty days of his life while at his residence in New Wye, Appalachia, U.S.A., according to Charles Kinbote, the editor and commentator on Shade's poem (12). But the novel *Pale Fire* is also the poem by Shade plus a fantastic, and fantastically detailed, "Foreword," "Commentary," and "Index" composed by Kinbote (born July 5, 1915; died October 19, 1959) during the last month or so of his life at Cedarn, Utana, on the Idoming border in the West of the United States. And the novel is also at least three stories that are inextricably intertwined.

Many novels are built on many levels, but *Pale Fire* is particularly complex. The first hurdle is point of view: the novel would seem to be given purely by Kinbote, except for the poem by Shade; but Kinbote himself may not always be the same person. However, in its most apparent terms, the story is that of the "I," the scholar Charles

Kinbote, teacher of Zemblan (the language and literature of the country, Zembla) at Wordsmith University in New Wye, Appalachia; but, according to Miss McCarthy, Kinbote is really V. Botkin, an "American scholar of Russian descent," who is mentioned only in the novel's "Index." Kinbote is the neighbor and great admirer of the American poet, John Shade, who is a kind of shadow of Robert Frost; for Shade reports in a television discussion of poetry that "my name/Was mentioned twice, as usual just behind/ (one oozy footstep) Frost" (48). Shade's major poem, "Pale Fire," written in those couplets, shares formal relationships with Frost's poetry; and most of Shade's minor poems that are cited in Kinbote's commentary are also formally traditional. But Shade is not Frost — he is much closer to Nabokov, who also writes a traditionally shaped poetry, both in Russian and English: for Shade and Nabokov are forever connecting things.

During the "present" of the novel, between July 5 and July 21, 1959, Shade is writing the poem which, if conventional on one level, is also a rather brilliant personal poem, an excellent poem, in its own right. It is not a "confession" in the Allen Ginsberg manner; but Shade does give some of his life — his childhood, his marriage, the story of the suicide of his ugly-duckling daughter, and his own searches for the meaning of life and death. But he is always the poet who is aware that he is making an object, not simply taking part in a process or undertaking a self-cure. And, as Page Stegner remarks, although, and because, the poem is filled with "numerous parodies and echoes of other poems and poets, [it] is not a joke . . . [but] a serious meditation on death, [on] the patterns of fate that suggest an imaginative consciousness on the other side of death, and [so on] the artist's escape from the consequences of physical deformity and decay into the realms of pure aesthetic delight — his poetic sensibility."[2]

All the time that Shade is writing, Kinbote is observing him, covertly and openly, even to the point of window peeping. For Kinbote is also telling Shade a wild and improbable story about the last king of Zembla; Kinbote thinks Shade should make, and is making, his poem about this king's life, escape from Zembla, and present existence. This story of Charles Xavier Vseslav, "surnamed The Beloved" (306), is given the reader largely in the "Commentary." The title that Kinbote wishes Shade to give his poem is "Solus Rex" — the title, as I have observed, that Nabokov actually gave to his unfinished novel about the king of a small island country (and which is, we should remember, a chess term).

It is "obvious" that Kinbote is mad; that he is forcing himself upon Shade; and that, although Shade seems to like Kinbote, his wife, Sybil, can barely tolerate their eccentric, homosexual neighbor. However, on July 21, 1959, when she is away, Shade, having finished his poem, accepts Kinbote's offer of a drink. But waiting for them at Kinbote's house is a madman named Jack Grey who, confusing Shade with the Judge Goldsworth from whom Kinbote has rented the house, shoots Shade, who dies instantly. Sybil Shade, arriving, finds her husband dead and is led to believe that Kinbote tried to save him. In her grief and gratitude, she is trapped by Kinbote into allowing him to be the editor of Shade's poem, "Pale Fire".

Kinbote has already discovered that the poem is not what he thought Shade was writing. Nevertheless, since he feels it is somehow telling his story, he flees West with the manuscript cards. There, in a run down "motor lodge," Kinbote writes his foreword, commentary, and index; but he tells his own "story" about Charles Xavier Vseslav in the guise of editing the poem.

Kinbote's story of Charles Xavier Vseslav is the main body of the novel. A fascinating, insane, and Nabokovian story, it contains perhaps more of Nabokov and of the actual world than perhaps either Kinbote or Nabokov would admit. As Alfred Appel has stated, "The figure of the exile embodies the human condition in our time";[3] and, if Vladimir Nabokov as an American and a Russian is no longer an exile, Charles Kinbote is in his madness — and so is Charles Xavier Vseslav, the Beloved, the last and maybe the only true king of that distant Northern land, Zembla. The name "Zembla," Kinbote rather too neatly explains, and so gives us two of the major themes of the novel: the theme of the lost land (Zembla, Russia), and the problem of what is real and what is not. Zembla, Kinbote says, is not derived from the Russian *zemlya*, meaning "earth," "land," with overtones of "homeland," but from "Semblerland, a land of reflections, of 'resemblers' " (265). However, both derivations are true.

Therefore, by bits and patches, we are given the history of Zembla; the biographies of Charles' ancestors, many of them mad or imbecilic in the proper royal tradition; and the confessions of Charles himself — again by indirection, for Kinbote always uses the third person when talking of Charles, except in the very last part of the book. For dynastic reasons, Charles is finally married to Disa, Duchess of Payn, of Great Payn and Mone (a rather too weak joke); but the marriage is never consummated since Charles, like Kinbote, is homosexual. Queen Disa, who loves Charles despite his disability, finally wearies of the torture of competing with his harem of lovely page boys and, leaving Zembla, settles on the Côte d'Azur.

She is safe there when a revolution led by the Extremists (Communists related to *Bend Sinister's* Ekwilists) breaks out. Charles is trapped; but he manages to escape after a mild yet threatening imprisonment due to the revolutionaries' wanting the secret of where the crown jewels are hidden. In a reprise of Victor Wind's daydream and Pnin's sleeping dream, Charles flees across the Bera Mountains to the seacoast where he is whisked out of the country by boat, first to France, and then to America. In disguise to escape his pursuing enemies, he is given a job teaching Zemblan at Wordsmith University. Charles is, of course, Charles Kinbote.

But within these stories of Kinbote, the Shades, and Charles the Beloved, Kinbote is telling yet another story — the history of the final journey of the infamous Jakob Gradus, who was born July 5, 1915, the same day as Shade and the same day and year as Charles. Gradus, while in jail, commits suicide with a safety razor blade a few days after the murder of John Shade. For Jakob Gradus' aliases not only include Jack Degree, de Grey, d'Argus (familiar name for Nabokov readers), Vinogradus, but also Jack Grey (and part of Nabokov). As Jakob Gradus, he is not the madman who kills John Shade by mistake; instead, he is a petty revolutionary who has been made the instrument of a group of powerful and secret Zemblan Extremists, the so-called Shadows, who send him on his assassination journey. As an assassin, Gradus is a failure, just as he has been a failure all his life; and his being a failure is the "true" reason for his suicide.

All of the stories are effectively and economically, if somewhat obscurely, introduced in the first three notes of Kinbote's commentary. If we look back at the stories with our eye on "what happens next?", we have to agree with Miss McCarthy that Kinbote is not only mad but that he is "really" V. Botkin and is making up his stories. Indeed, when a questioner asks Kinbote if his name is not "a kind of anagram of Botkin or Botkine," he replies, defensively and sarcastically, that he is being confused "with some refugee from Nova Zembla" (267). Miss McCarthy adds, however, that "each plane or level in . . . [the novel's] shadow box proves to be a false bottom."[4]

My point is that each level is quite as true as the next. The novel is an order within itself, an esthetic order created by the *whole* novel.

What the events are, on the deepest level, is the author's vision of the world, a vision that makes the world one. In *Speak, Memory*, Nabokov talks of the poet's experiencing in one moment of time "an instantaneous and transparent organism of events, of which [he] . . . sitting in a lawn chair, at Ithaca, N.Y. . . . is the nucleus."[5] On a purely external level, *Pale Fire* is a parody and a satire of pedantic and sometimes inaccurate editors and critics. Vladimir Nabokov even wryly mocks Vladimir Nabokov, in particular his procedure in his translation and annotation of Pushkin's *Eugene Onegin*, a work published after but completed before *Pale Fire*, and a work of consummate and accurate, if sometimes eccentric, scholarship. On the other hand, *Pale Fire* is a defense of pedantic editors, for the defense is both a way of literature and a way of life. As John O. Lyons states, Nabokov's "narrative method . . . is the examination of a text (or vision of aesthetic order) by some real or imagined artist who vies with God in disordering a universe."[6] However, the text and the universe come together, if well read.

Nabokov stated in an interview that Kinbote asserts that parody is the "last resort of wit," certainly not he himself [7]; but the person who did say this (true, the words are given through Kinbote) was John Shade — who says it ironically; for he is praising parody: "I have a certain liking, I admit,/For Parody, that last resort of wit" (269). My argument is that Nabokov's voice, in creating his artists, expresses both his anti-selves and himself. I have quoted him as saying "Satire is a lesson, parody is a game," and he means that literature is a game but a serious game. Moreover, Nabokov wrote that both in art and science "there is no delight without the detail[s], and . . . unless these are thoroughly understood and remembered, all 'general ideas' (so easily acquired, so profitably resold) must necessarily remain but worn passports allowing their bearers short cuts from one area of ignorance to another."[8]

Therefore, in its entirety, *Pale Fire* is a complex, detailed, ordered, and comic novel of 315 pages in the Putnam edition; it is divided into the magical literary number of three parts; it was composed by Vladimir Nabokov during his sixth and perhaps some of his seventh decade; and it was published as his fifth English novel in 1962. The novel is also what Andrew Field has called it, "one of the eight masterpieces of the novel in this century (Nabokov is the only author who has written *two* of them!)"[9] In its vision of mankind and in its complexity and yet its simplicity of design, the novel is, if not a masterpiece, a serious and beautifully designed work. If the novel is serious, it is also comic in its picture of the modern world. Nabokov himself, though, suggests that the comic and the cosmic "sides of things" differ only by "one sibilant" and that a literary work's true function is to show us how "the mysteries of the irrational" are "perceived through rational words."[10]

The novel presents the irrational through the rational by probing the world of madness; but I must emphasize that it is neither a psychological nor a sociological case study. It works, as a Nabokov novel always works, by indirection — not by the author's telling us his narrator is mad, but rather by having the narrator, Kinbote, unwittingly unveil himself while creating at the same moment that work of art which connects worlds. It is Kinbote who says that the poem "Pale Fire" is a strange work whose "underside of the weave . . . entrances the beholder and only begetter, whose past intercoils there with the fate of the innocent author" (17). He thus likens Shade to Shakespeare and himself to Shakespeare's Mr. W. H. — or to Thomas Thorpe's — since the Shakespearean facts are unclear. Kinbote lets us know that his grasp on "reality" is most tenuous; but, at the same time, he shows us levels of reality and also introduces his own creator and his past; for Nabokov is the beholder, the only begetter, and the not so innocent author of the poem and of the novel.

Correspondingly, John Shade argues that we should not call a certain old man a "loony" since "One should not apply . . . [loony] to a person who deliberately peels off a drab and unhappy past and replaces it with a brilliant invention. That's merely turning a new leaf with the left hand" (238). The woman to whom Shade has been speaking says, "John calls him [the old man] a fellow poet," which, of course, he is. Just before this reported interchange, Kinbote has written — in a fine revision of the epitaphal "Et in Arcadia ego" — " 'Even in Arcady am I,' says Dementia"; and he also replies to the woman's assertion with "We all are, in a sense, poets, Madam" (237 - 38). For the mad Kinbote is a poet who entwines pasts. Kinbote, then, is one more artist figure. He has failed, perhaps, but he is creative nevertheless in the same way that Humbert Humbert was. Moreover, Kinbote is also oddly appealing, like Humbert Humbert and unlike Hermann Karlovich.

Therefore, if Kinbote, paraphrasing Hamlet, hints that he will commit suicide in order to escape all his worlds (220 - 22) and if Nabokov tells us authoritatively that he did so on the day that "happens to be both the anniversary of Pushkin's *Lyceum* and that of 'poor old man Swift's death,'[11] Nabokov is doing more than associating Kinbote with yet another madman, Swift. He is associating Kinbote with other writers, Swift and Pushkin; and he is showing us how Shade's, Kinbote's, and Nabokov's *Pale Fire* is both literature and part of literature at the same time that it is a kind of tragedy, an imitation of the struggle against man's fate.

All of this ordered complexity comes together in John Shade's lines which comment both on the novel in which he appears and on our actual world. The "contrapuntal theme" of our existence is

> Just this: not text, but texture; not the dream
> But topsy-turvical coincidence,
> Not flimsy nonsense, but a web of sense.
> Yes! It sufficed that I in life could find
> Some kind of link-and-bobolink, some kind
> Of correlated pattern in the game,
> Plexed artistry, and something of the same
> Pleasure in it as they who played it found. (63)

However, "art at its greatest is fantastically deceitful and complex," Nabokov holds;[12] and the true shape for *Pale Fire* perhaps can be taken from two of its own images. The first image is the moment that Charles the Beloved, king of Zembla, escapes from his imprisonment in his palace in Onhava, Zembla, and passes a man reading a newspaper: the man's face has been destroyed by an explosion in a glass factory (no doubt where mirrors were made); and "all the art of plastic surgery had only resulted in a hideous tesselated texture with parts of pattern and parts of outline seeming to change, to fuse or to separate, like fluctuating cheeks and chins in a distortive mirror" (146). But the man suddenly reveals himself to be one of the king's supporters, Odon or Donald O'Donnell; and his terrible face is only a false mask, a "varicolored semi-transparent film" (146 - 47). We must not assume that Odon, unmasked, is necessarily more "real" than the mask he has put on; for he is in Kinbote's world — and, too, he has a true double, his half-brother, Nodo (this reversed spelling of names is everywhere), who is the son of their father, Leopold O'Donnell, "and of a Zemblan boy impersonator" (311) — a mad, comic, and unsettling reversal of the Elizabethan boys playing female parts or of our modern female impersonators. The second image is in the first lines of Shade's poem, "I was the shadow of the waxwing slain/By the false azure in the window-pane" (33). The "world" of *Pale Fire* is not only filled with shadows but comprised of shadows; and the delusive azure, blue, is the will of the wisp that leads the characters into their intricate and insane dances.

But, as I have said in the Introduction to this book, the major image of the novel, finally, is the spiral. If Mary McCarthy speaks of the "burden" of *Pale Fire* as being "love,"[13] and if Andrew Field responds that "life and death are at the center of . . . [the novel], with love and sex merely decoy or secondary motifs — poetic metaphors of the primary theme,"[14] I must assert again that Nabokov *is* speaking of love and of life and of death through his love for language and his artistic structure. He is writing about all the things in the universe that language can create — almost everything except, perhaps, the final mystery.

Pale Fire is, then, about Nabokov's loves — language and memory (or timelessness) — and about "American and European" things. In a note, Kinbote (who is a spiral image of John Shade and of Nabokov himself) remarks upon Shade's lines about the dying exile who "conjures in two tongues": "English and Zemblan, etc.," Kinbote says, repeating "English and Russian" four times in sixteen sets of "English and. . . ." He ends, of course, with a seventeenth: "American and European" (235). The Zemblan language that Kinbote speaks, although based upon a Teutonic grammar, has a Teutonic and Russian vocabulary (like that of *Bend Sinister*), and this language, a verbal blending of Nabokov's American and European worlds, is "the tongue of the mirror" (242).

Not only do the stories and subject matters give us meanings, but the actual shape of the novel has its significance. That shape suggests the spiral, the image of time both unchanged and changing, of the past both lost and yet still existent. The Foreword which introduces the novel was written after the rest, at least in the fictive world — for we can only guess as to what the actual author wrote first. The poem, which comes second, was written first; and the notes, which come last, were written second. They are then in a three-one-two order (although the notes sometimes refer us back to the Foreword, implying that the Foreword was not written after *all* the notes). In brief, all times are made one in the work of art. The title poem also has its spiral shape and its literary — man's — vision of his condition: "*Man's life as commentary to abstruse/Unfinished poem. Note for further use*" (67), Shade writes. But, as in all mirror-image worlds — such as Sudarg of Bokay's, Gradus of Yakob's, and d'Argus' of Nabokov's — the statement can and must be reversed: "*Man's poem as commentary to abstruse/Unfinished life.*" Topsy-

turvy coincidence — not text, not message, not sociological rappor-
tage — is what Nabokov is representing.

The first canto begins with the line, "I was the shadow of the waxwing slain/By the false azure in the windowpane." If John Shade
opens his poem with an image of a reflection in which the real and
the mirrored become one, the purpose is that of the scene in *Speak,
Memory* in which Nabokov and his mother, playing cards on a train,
are reflected in the window and are superimposed, therefore, upon
the scene outside.[15] Art and actuality become one. The poem, within
its 999 lines, contains past, present, and perhaps future. The first
canto of 166 lines treats Shade's early life, but it includes certain
trances which seem to hint of something more than this life. The second canto of 334 lines is mostly devoted to the sad life and death of
Hazel Shade. The third canto, in which Shade meditates upon death
and tells the story of a kind of heart attack in which he had a vision
that suggests an existence beyond death, has 334 lines also. The last
canto, which brings the chronological line of Shade's poem and his
life up to the present, is a truncated 165 lines, ending with the un-
rhymed word "lane." We can only suppose, as Kinbote supposes,
that the final line would repeat the first line, starting a new spiral.
Everything has changed from the first line, but it contains within
itself the future, the death of Shade and the death of Kinbote, as well
as the suggestion of timelessness.

I have pointed out this play of relationships already in the names
of Nabokov's characters; *Pale Fire* is made up of such connectings.
Shade's name leads all the rest. The chief Extremists are Shadows,
for instance. But one of the hidden wordplays brings the name and
the mirror images precisely together. Kinbote speaks of the
"anonymous [Zemblan] masterpiece," the *Kongs-skugg-sio*, a title
he translates as *The Royal Mirror* (76). *Kongs* is Zemblan for
"king's" or "royal"; *skugg* is Zemblan for "mirror." But we find that
there is a Swedish word *skugga* which means *shade* or *shadow*.
Shade is mirror, both are the king's, and the two are nearly one.

Gerald Emerald, Shade's and Kinbote's youthful colleague,
dresses in "a cheap green jacket" (268); he is repeated by
Izumrudov, one of the important Shadows, who appears once
dressed in a green velvet jacket (255). Not too surprisingly, *izumrud*
is Russian for "emerald, smaragdite." And there are dozens of plays
on "azure, blue, ultramarine" in English, in Russian, and in French.
Miss McCarthy suggests that the pattern in Nabokov's use of colors
is to associate them with certain people and perhaps with certain

moral judgments.[16] To me, this pattern is not one that makes divisions; it is one of surprise, one that demonstrates that good and evil characters are connected by the same colors, that good and evil are not that easily distinguished. The same pattern applies to the names: Shade is part of the Shadows; Odon has his wicked half-brother Nodo; Baron Radomir Mandevil has, in another reverse-spelled name, his wicked cousin Baron Mirador Mandevil. The "man-devil" play in this name is obvious, as well as the allusion to Sir John de Mandeville, the classic liar-creator who sometimes told truths.

Names, colors, numbers are shades or shadows of others, a repetition in an altered form. The title of *Pale Fire* comes from *Timon of Athens*, act 4, scene 3:

> The sun's a thief, and with his great attraction
> Robs the vast sea; the moon's an arrant thief,
> And her pale fire she snatches from the sun.

Miss McCarthy, explaining the meaning of the thief imagery in the novel, says that *Pale Fire* is about many kinds of theft, including literary theft.[17] This is true. But we must notice that the image from Shakespeare is that of a cycle, a movement from one thing to another, not exactly but nearly circular, for different things are stolen. The image is the extension of the *marrowsky* into the spiral. And such a pattern sometimes reverses things in order to show that they are not simple. Kinbote tries to remember certain lines from *Timon*, but he does not have the English with him and has to translate back from the Zemblan. He is quoting the passage just cited, but he so changes it in "translation" that we can hardly recognize it:

> The sun is a thief: she lures the sea
> and robs it. The moon is a thief:
> he steals his silvery light from the sun.
> The sea is a thief: it dissolves the moon. (80)

The "pale fire" disappears; but, more important, the genders of the sun and moon are reversed. Gender, as always in Nabokov, is an ambiguous thing — we have only to remember the story of Nodo's mother, the *boy* impersonator. But sex is ambiguous because Nabokov is attacking the clear, divisive, and perhaps untrue categories of simple common sense. The artistic pattern is like the pattern of the universe: a thing exists, but it is not simple; for it looks different from a different position. Reversals and coincidences are not chance alone; for, as Nabokov says, "In a sense, all poetry is positional: to try to express one's position in regard to the universe embraced by consciousness, is an immemorial urge. The arms of consciousness reach out and grope, and the longer they are the better."[18] And so it is ambiguously ironic when Charles Kinbote who is V. Botkin and by means of a *marrowsky* V. Nabokov claims, "I have no desire to twist and batter an unambiguous *apparatus criticus* into the monstrous semblance of a novel" (86).

"Semblance," of course, is the key word. Shade points out that "resemblances are the shadows of differences" (265). And, too, he speaks of "playing a game of worlds" (63) — of worlds — and words. And later in a rejected draft, Shade remarks of his name: "Shade, *Ombre*, almost 'man'/In Spanish . . ." (174). In thus linking himself with the universal, he is not a symbol of man; he is a man — and, therefore, he is related to all others. But the pun is also a statement that art and life are intricately close, almost one.

And so "all hangs together," as Nabokov holds in "An Evening of Russian Poetry." But, at the same time, everything is different. For an example of how the art work shows relationships as well as differences, we can take Shade's statement to his wife Sybil in his poem about the four thousand times her pillow "has been creased/By our two heads" (43). Kinbote remarks in a note that, in the morning hours of July 5, 1959, he observed the Shades' house; and, seeing the light on in their bedroom, he "smiled indulgently, for, according to my deductions, only two nights had passed since the three-thousand-nine-hundred-ninety-ninth time — but no matter" (157). Kinbote is writing this note after reading the poem, but he is speaking of his thoughts on a night when he could not have known what Shade had written. In short, he knew what was going on in Shade's house because he is, in a real sense, Shade — although neither Page Stegner's suggestion that "the entire story including the poem is a fabrication of the artist-madman Kinbote is not too farfetched"[19] nor Andrew Field's argument that "there are many compellingly logical reasons to place John Shade before Charles Kinbote"[20] is quite right. Each statement limits the work to being the expression of a character within it and each limits the connections that the work makes.

Finally, then, we must return to Nabokov, for it is he who is mak-

ing the art work and so the connections. Since all does hang
together, therefore,

> My back is Argus-eyed. I live in danger.
> False shadows turn to track me as I pass
> and, wearing beards, disguised as secret agents,
>   . . . warily they linger
> or silently approach the door and ring
> the bell of memory and run away.[21]

The speaker is Nabokov, Argus, Gradus — all his characters — who
are pursued by shadow or shades that are his own memories. But
these memories are out of time; it is himself who pursues himself.
And behind him, in Russia, the speaker says that he leaves a
kingdom, a kingdom that is of language, not of political power. He is
Kinbote the exiled king, Kinbote who translates his name as regicide
or "king's destroyer," for "a king who sinks his identity in the mirror
of exile is in a sense just that" (267). But the name of Kinbote is also
related to the Anglo-Saxon *cyn* which means "kind" or "relative"
and to *bote* which means "reward." He has been paid back in a
sense, or in kind. "I have lost a sceptre," the speaker of the poem
says. But Charles Kinbote announces, "You will never find our
crown, necklace and sceptre" (244), for they are too well hidden. In
the Index of *Pale Fire*, the reader is sent from "Crown Jewels" to
"Hiding Place" to "Potaynik" to "Taynik" which is Russian for
"secret place." But the word *Taynik* also introduces a common Russian phrase that means "the secret recesses of the heart." The sceptre, then, which is one of language, still exists in the heart and
memory of the speaker. It still exists, for everything that was still is.
Everything exists and is related, just as the points on all segments of
a spiral.

The poem "Pale Fire" is, in reality, the work of Vladimir
Nabokov. He gives it to a fictional character named John Shade. But
Shade is Nabokov's American disguise, the other half or third of
Nabokov's world. We must remember that, when Nabokov speaks of
his Russian, his Western Europe, and his American worlds, he says
that he "invented" them.[22] He invented them in two senses of the
word: first, he discovered them; second, he fabricated them. At the
end of *Pale Fire*, Kinbote alone does not say: "I shall continue
to exist. I may assume other disguises. . . . I may turn up yet, on
another campus, as an old, happy, healthy, heterosexual Russian, a
writer in exile, . . ." an "old Russian" who may write a play "with

three principles" (not principals, but *principles*): "a lunatic who intends to kill an imaginary king, another lunatic who imagines himself to be that king, and a distinguished old poet who stumbles by chance into the line of fire, and perishes in the clash between the two figments" (300 - 301). We cannot doubt that Nabokov is talking about his own work — or that the figments are quite real.

The writer is saying once more that the same pattern may be repeated — although changed. Nabokov's belief in spirality is not, it must be emphasized, deterministic. There is freedom in that belief, just as there is order but also freedom in art. Toward the end of *Speak, Memory*, Nabokov recurs to the image and says that, "if, in the spiral unwinding of things, space warps into something akin to time, and time, in its turn, warps into something akin to thought, then, surely, another dimension follows" — a dimension that could be better "unless spirals become vicious circles again."[23]

II   Ada

Sometimes, in the spiral unwinding of things in art, another dimension does follow; that is, life imitates art, and our solid reality trembles under our feet. In *Pale Fire* (1962), the fictional John Francis Shade writes: "Space is a swarming in the eyes; and time,/A singing in the ears" (40). Shade is, for the moment, examining the possibility, the probability, that something more than our time and our place exists — that time and space may be mere tricks of our senses. And so, "Why/Scorn a hereafter none can verify/. . ./?" (41). In 1964, the actual American popularizer of scientific ideas, Martin Gardner, published the book *The Ambidextrous Universe* which is an attempt to explain to the layman the meaning of certain modern concepts in physics. Gardner discusses the possibility that anti-matter and anti-worlds have their own space and time. He examines mirror worlds, doubles, right and left handedness, and backspelled names that are the same as frontspelled ones — or, in other words, the madly sane world of modern physics as well as of Lewis Carroll's *Through the Looking Glass*, Nabokov's *Pale Fire*, and human existence. "Space and time," Gardner says, "are like the two lenses in a pair of glasses. Without the glasses we could see nothing. . . . We experience only our sensory perceptions: what we see, hear, feel, smell, taste. These perceptions are, in a sense, illusions." He then cites John Shade's lines as illustration; and he adds a facetious footnote attributing them only to Shade, not to Nabokov.[24] The fictional creature has usurped the creator's place — but, too, all truth is made hypothetical.

In 1969, Nabokov published *Ada or Ardor: A Family Chronicle,*[25] a novel that contains another title within itself, *Van's Book,* which is Nabokov in anagram so that the author is an integral part of his own work. *Ada* is, as Alfred Appel says, "the first and only classic of Amerussian literature,"[26] a literature that Nabokov invented. Nabokov's novel presents the world Antiterra or Demonia in which a lovely, romantic Russia is located in North America; this country is side by side and intermingled with a Canada named Estoty or Estotiland, where a variety of languages are spoken without furor or competition. Both countries are part of "America." In that invented world, Tartary, a rather savage state, covers much of the Eastern hemisphere; it is located approximately where the Soviet Union and China exist in *our* reality. Nabokov only admits our actuality by having his hero, Van Veen, recognize that our earth, Terra, really exists and that, at the moment, in Terra, "Russian peasants and poets" are not in an imaginative, free place called Estotiland (582). Other Nabokov novels could also be called "Amerussian," but *Ada* is his most explicit attempt to bring together in a work of the imagination those places and experiences that made him an artist. If *Ada* does not quite succeed as a novel, it fails as does the later *Look at the Harlequins!;* for these two novels tend to be more about Nabokov's theme of the artist than realized works of art in themselves.

As a classic of Amerussian literature which is about humankind in space and time as well as about the artist, *Ada* begins with a thematic sentence, a mirror image, of a famous literary line which is the first sentence of Tolstoy's *Anna Karenina:* "All happy families are more or less dissimilar; all unhappy ones are more or less alike" (3), and develops from there. The events that take place in this science-fiction mirror world are narrated straightforwardly enough, even if deceptively so. In large part, they are told chronologically, although the writer-protagonist, Van Veen, is recording his life story toward the end of his very long existence; and he necessarily colors these events as he looks back. The novel is, therefore, a rather traditional one, despite its subject matter. But it is also new, for Van's discussion of what time is as well as his "autobiography" that makes and finds those "combinational delights" which delight Nabokov creates a novel that is both new and old. Like Nabokov, Van is "not quite a savant, but completely an artist" whose "originality of literary style constitutes the only real honesty of a writer" (471).

The novel, then, purports to be the memoir, the shaped autobiography — indeed, the *Speak Memory* — of Van Veen. For Van perceives his work and life, as Nabokov seems to perceive his, as

"a match between Inspiration and Design" (578), and as "an ample
and delightful chronicle, whose principal part is staged in a dream-
bright America — for are not our childhood memories comparable to
Vineland-born [sic] caravelles, indolently encircled by the white
birds of dreams?" (588). Van writes these words in the introduction
to a short retelling of his whole life on the last pages of his story. But
this mere reversal, as well as the retelling as though it were an "introduction," is a way of showing us that the work and the life are
shaped; and they are shaped, of course, as a spiral of time.

Van is seemingly the child of the marriage of a certain Dementiy
(Demon) and Aqua Durmanov Veen; but he is actually the son of
Demon and of Aqua's twin sister, Marina (whose name is a watery
anagram of that Hotel Mirana owned by Humbert Humbert's
father). Marina later marries Daniel Veen, Demon's cousin (the two
men and the two sisters have common ancestors); and she bears two
more children. The first of these, Ada, is also the child of Demon;
the younger, Lucette, is Dan's. The lifelong love affair of Van and
Ada is the central story which Van relates, largely in the third person. Ada contributes notes which are incorporated by Ronald
Oranger, the manuscript's editor, who also adds a few items himself,
including the absurd, parodistic, and innocent introductory disclaimer. The memoir is published, as the disclaimer says, after Van's
death. And so there is one more deliberate echo of Nabokov's earlier
novels, such as *Despair, Lolita,* and *Pale Fire;* the dead narrator confesses his crimes or at least his sins and so becomes the past alive in
the present through art.

The novel is divided into five parts, but the structure is not dependent upon the action. Each part is shorter than the previous part;
and the fourth part is mostly Van's essay, "The Texture of Time,"
which tells little of the story. The first part presents most of the story
— and the satire. In this parody of the "bildungsroman," we have,
first, the history of the hero's ancestors, these trilingual, rich, upper-
class Veen-Durmanovs ("durman" is Russian for "narcotic," a word
play that characterizes); and, second, the introduction of the sensitive, young-boy hero when he first meets his cousin-sister at Ardis
Hall ("ardis" is Greek for the "point of an arrow," and this play, too,
echoes throughout the novel) when he is fourteen and a half and she
is twelve. Van and Ada fall almost immediately into love and, almost
as immediately, into each other's arms; their sexual relationships are
athletic and repetitious and no doubt spiced by the soon-discovered
secret that they are not just cousins.

Ada shares Nabokov's interest in and knowledge about the natural world; Van, although more physical than Humbert Humbert or Charles Kinbote, is only interested because Ada is. Van's passions are more intellectual; it is he who becomes interested in the hypothesis, almost a religious belief, of the possible sister-planet Terra. Because Ada, his supposed cousin, is actually his sister and, even more, his enantiomorph — for she has the same small brown spot on the back of her left hand that he has on his right one — we know that "incest" is not only an anagram of "insect" but a form of doubling which suggests the attraction and the mystery of worlds.

Ardis Hall is reached from the "half-Russian village" of Gamlet, which is Hamlet (character and hamlet) in Russian disguise. At Ardis, Van meets his former governess-teacher, Mlle. Ida (Belle) Lariviere, now Lucette's governess. The twist is that Mlle. Lariviere is a writer whose pen name is Guillaume de Montparnasse and whose most famous story is "The Necklace," or "La Riviere de Diamants," which is of course a Nabokov-Sebastian Knight transformation of Guy de Maupassant's "La Parure" or "The Diamond Necklace." The novel is a cornucopia of literary and historical parodies that range from Cavalcanti through Gerard de Nerval through Tolstoy (a major figure) through Warren Gamaliel Harding through T. S. Eliot, through Heinrich Müller, who is Henry Miller, through. . . . The parodies mock *poshlust* ("false literary and social values") at the same moment that they preserve true values; but they also bring into our consciousness as readers and as social beings the whole of human experience. In its way, then, *Ada* is a kind of encyclopedia; more so even than *Pale Fire*, it is a work that, in Northrop Frye's definition, is "a total body tending to incorporate itself in a single encyclopedic form."[27] We can only connect by including everything, including its opposite.

But Nabokov parodies even himself, both to assure us that we cannot take him too seriously and to add another level of meaning as well as fun: Marina is to take part in a movie called *Les Enfants Maudits*, a shot at Jean Cocteau's *Les Enfants Terribles* (once more the incest theme); but the original film story of *Les Enfants Maudits* is a mocking of Nabokov, for it is the story of Van and Ada — doubleness turned upon itself too far is more than parody, though; it can be a kind of insanity.

The first section of the novel ends with the discovery by Van, now a young adult, that his beloved Ada has been unfaithful to him, not once but many times. In anger and despair, he picks a quarrel with an innocent man, almost seeking his own death. However, Van is merely wounded; and the lovers are separated for some four years. In this time, he publishes his only novel, *Letters from Terra*, under the pen name of Voltemand, a name which takes us back to *Hamlet*. Van believes and does not believe in Terra; his science fiction novel, like Nabokov's science-fiction one, is also an examination of the frightening possibility that Terra is a much more violent place than Antiterra; its history, in fact, in Van's hands becomes much like that of our earth. But Van's history of Terra only comes up to 1940; everything else is blank.

Van's life in these years is filled with love affairs, mostly physical and insensitive ones, and with his writing. In 1892, he and Ada meet again, but their reunion is a short-lived one; for their father, by a concatenation of apparently fortuitous events — one of those series of linked actions which Nabokov uses to suggest both inevitability and pure chance — discovers them living together. Van, with a kind of guilt, insists they part — and then he imagines that he commits suicide, an act that parodies the failed suicide of Smurov, the central character of *The Eye*. Nabokov's purpose in both cases is to show that our memories of our past lives may be simple fabrications made up for us or by us; that we may all have committed suicide yesterday; and that our lives, as we remember them, are acts of artistic creation, not something necessary.

Van returns to his sexual and intellectual pursuits; Ada marries Andrey Vinelander, "a Greek-Catholic" Russian descendant of the discoverers of America, a nice parody of discoverers. For, if, in Antiterra, Russians, not Scandinavians, were the first Europeans to see America and to call it Vineland, and if the Gulf of Mexico was first sighted by men from West Africa, we are meant to see that Nabokov discovered the whole of his world and that artistic creation makes worlds, not simple voyages. Ada and her husband live on an Arizona ranch, along with Andrey's vicious and intellectually pretentious sister who is this novel's believer in Freudianism or, in Antiterra, in the ideas of Dr. Froit of Signy-Mondieu-Mondieu.

Van's investigations of terrology and of time make him a respected scholar, despite his being an artist, not a philosopher. But his personal life continues to be horrible. His and Ada's half-sister, Lucette, who has been all her life in love with him, boards the same ship that he is taking back to the United States. He, desperately wishing to avoid incest with another of his sisters, rejects her brutally; and she commits suicide by jumping off the ship. Lucette is a parody of doubleness, the half-sister who is not the perfect double, and who may be, then, a positive. For her name contains "light," just as Ada's contains "hell" ("ad" is Russian for "hell," derived from the Greek "Hades").

When Ada and Van meet again in 1905, they decide to ignore law and custom in order to live together; but at this moment — again by one of those trick and neat coincidences so patently absurd as to be a deliberate part of the design that Nabokov delights in — Andrey Vinelander is discovered to be dying; and Ada returns to him. But Andrey Vinelander does not die until 1922; and not until then do Ada and Van finally settle down, this time for the rest of their lives. We should note that they meet both in 1905 and in 1922 in Mont Roux, Switzerland, which is, of course, Nabokov's actual home, Montreux. The two grow old, feeble, giving up sex, when Van is eighty-five; but they never give up their minds. He now writes his book, ending with a Part 5 that "is the true introduction of my ninety-seven percent true, and three percent likely, *Ada*" (567).

If Van's "aim was to compose a kind of novella in the form of a treatise on the Texture of Time," his is the reverse of the usual procedure since philosophers sometimes write treatises in the form of novellas. But Ada has the commonsense response to Van's attempt to define time: "I wonder if the attempt to discover those things is worth the stained glass. We can know the time, we can know a time. We can never know Time. Our senses are simply not meant to perceive it. It is like —" (562 - 63). Like what? We cannot know exactly, but it is like Van Veen's book; his treatise on time is only a chapter of the novel; for the actual novel is both introduced and ended in the actual story, which is the time and a time.

The devices of the novel — the science-fiction aspect (a number of Nabokov's novels are formally "science fiction") — are not ways of escaping time or of escaping our world. The time "lag," for instance, between our world and Antiterra is a device for examining time, but it also brings Antiterra's history, its existence, into consonance with ours and yet allows it to still exist as something separate — as an act of the author's imagination. Van was born in 1870, Antiterra time; but he writes his memoir between 1957 and 1967 and so is contemporary with us — his advanced age allows the past to be made part of the present. And, if Antiterra's history seems much less violent than ours, it still reflects ours, as mirrors do. For example, Van can say, approvingly, to his father, "That's very black of you, Dad" (241); and in this fashion he mocks and mimes American racism, American history as expressed in the cliché, "That's white of you."

Van, who is the universe's first and only true "anti-hero," receives therefore on his eighth birthday the book *Alice in the Camera Obscura* and so is gifted with worlds; that title contains Nabokov's worlds, his art, and his interests. Van, even though his first name is actually Ivan, shares initials as well as certain interests if not a life with V. V. Nabokov. Indeed, Nabokov's distant ancestor, the Tartar prince Nabok, manages a momentary appearance in Antiterra. Ben Sirine, who also appears, is described as "an obscene ancient Arab, expounder of anagrammatic dreams" (344); he is, with changes, V. Sirin, the young Nabokov. Also included are some of Nabokov's images, the "argus," and his dates, "April 23," together with many of his own works: *Pale Fire* is the name of a horse, "Spring in Fialta" is a mere season in a place, and *Lolita* is a rather long but "very airy and ample, black skirt" (77). But once more, the novel is no confession; the echoes are a transcendence of experience.

And so Antiterra does exist, a place where electricity is an obscene word and where advanced technology is largely based on water (the classic four elements — earth, air, fire, and water — are organizing images in the novel). There are even magic carpets called "jikkers" which are banned but are used by adventurous children. The novel is, then, as Appel asserts, "a great fairy tale, a supremely original work of the imagination."[28] But, again, imagination for Nabokov is a form of memory, personal and literary; and Van Veen almost repeats Nabokov's own musings on the first pages of *Speak, Memory* about the "nothingness" which preceded our birth. He also quotes quite exactly Nabokov's English version of the first words of Pushkin's *Eugene Onegin*, but he does so, of course, without giving Nabokov a footnote (314, 317).

As the aging author, therefore, Van writes the treatise on time "The Texture of Time" in which he remarks: " 'Space is a swarming in the eyes, and Time a singing in the ears,' says John Shade, a modern poet, as quoted by an invented philosopher ('Martin Gardiner') in *The Ambidextrous Universe*, page 165" (542). In short, in Nabokov's world, his people are alive because they are his people; and the actual man of our world is reduced to being a mere invention, an imitation of the real. Plato is wrong, and art can do these things since it is one of the few ways, perhaps the only way, that man can control time and space, perhaps the only way he can *really* examine the *real*. As Ada says, "In 'real' life we are creatures of chance in an absolute void — unless we be artists ourselves" (426).

Art, Van-Nabokov says, is our expression of "something, which *until* expressed" has "only a twilight being. . . . It [is] the standing of a metaphor on its head not for the sake of the trick's difficulty, but in order to perceive an ascending waterfall or a sunrise in reverse: a triumph, in a sense, over the ardis of time" (184 - 85). Therefore, the author says, one can "surmise" that if Van and Ada Veen, in their late nineties, "ever intended to die they would die, as it were, *into* the finished book, into Eden or Hades [into *Ada — ad*, remember, is Russian for *hell*], into the prose of the book or the poetry of its blurb" (587). And so they do, as does Lolita, being at the last in art, out of our human time with its ambiguities.

Nevertheless, time, if separate from us as "objective time," is still only truly existent within us human beings; and, for Van and Nabokov, it is not neatly divided into past, present, and future. Instead, there are only two divisions, "the Past (ever-existing in my mind) and the Present (to which my mind gives duration and, therefore, reality)" (560).

But no imaginative author and no imaginative creature can remain logical. If Van remarks at one moment in his youth the "problems of space and time, space versus time, time-twisted space, space as time, time as space — and space breaking away from time, in the final tragic triumph of human cogitation: I am because I die" (153), he later cries out — in "The Texture of Time," a title that Nabokov once applied to his own novel before he finished it — to an imaginary heckler, "Who said *I* shall die?" (535). And he attempts to refute the heckler, to refute the future which contains "absolute necessities" — it occurs, we grow old, and we do die. And so he and Ada spend a morning just before Van's death "reworking their translation [into Russian] of a passage (lines 569 - 72) in John Shade's famous poem":

                              (. . . We give advice
To widower. He has been married twice:
He meets his wives, both loved, both loving, both
Jealous of one another. . . .)
(585 - 86)

Their choice of these lines, which describe a possible afterlife in which personalities and time continue, is their admission that all of us are, in brief, in time — we only overcome it in memory, which is art: "You lose your immortality when you lose your memory," Van says when he is fourteen; and he remembers the statement to record it when he is in his late nineties (584). For "time is but memory in the making" (559), he has already written.

Time and space which are necessity, time which is memory, and memory which is being human — these are the themes of all of Nabokov's works. But they are given to us in delight and in wonder. Still, as Van Veen says, "What a hoaxer, that old V. V.!" (56).

CHAPTER 9

Conclusion

A RT itself has been Vladimir Nabokov's subject in all of his work, but art in itself has not been the final purpose of his creative activity. He has created art in order to create his own and our lives. For Nabokov the act of creating art is mankind's most human act, its ordering of itself, and its giving purpose to itself. By the art act, man accepts but overcomes necessity, which is his existence in space and time. Nabokov has made his own life a part of his creative act in order to redeem time — to demonstrate that we are in time at the same moment that we can recover the past and so escape the tyranny of time.

Art, in ordering, makes a form. Nabokov's art is an art of language, and he is one of the great masters of language. It is through language that he has sought form and so meaning. His weaknesses as a novelist grow from his strength — he is sometimes too concerned with language and with pattern in themselves so that he sacrifices other elements of his work. He almost always creates interesting characters, for example, but he sometimes manipulates those characters for the sake of a formal connection within a work. He has said that writers who speak of their characters as taking over the work of art are abdicating their responsibilities as artists. But, if an author subordinates a particular aspect of his work to a larger design, he must be sure that the larger design does not violate the smaller element. Nabokov's best works — *Lolita, Pale Fire,* and *The Gift* — are successful structures as well as humanly alive novels that reward the reader on many levels. *Pnin,* which is less structurally complete, is very nearly one of his best works because of the liveliness of Pnin himself. Indeed, very few of Nabokov's other novels are real failures since his stories and his characters are always alive. These successes and failures of Nabokov are always a matter of degree.

Nabokov has, however, most probably already written his best works; for his last three novels — *Ada, Transparent Things,* and *Look at the Harlequins!* — have nearly been allegories of his life as an artist; and allegories are never equal to the actual thing. No doubt, too, his reputation will not remain at the level that it is at the moment. In a sense he is the last of the great modernist writers, and his reputation will suffer as the present reaction continues to grow against modernism and its concern with form. But Nabokov's major novels will remain essential parts of our literature, for he has created a body of work that is both esthetically and humanly satisfying.

Notes and References

Preface

1. "An Interview with Vladimir Nabokov," conducted by Alfred Appel, Jr., in *Nabokov: The Man and His Work*, ed. L. S. Dembo (Madison, Wisconsin, 1967), p. 32.

2. *Strong Opinions* (New York, 1973), p. 193.

3. Vladislav Khodasevich, "On Sirin," in *TriQuarterly*, 17 (Winter 1970), 96.

4. "Playboy Interview: Vladimir Nabokov," *Playboy*, 11 (January 1964), 40.

5. *Nikolai Gogol*, (Norfolk, Connecticut, 1944), p. 140.

6. Aleksandr Pushkin, *Eugene Onegin, A Novel in Verse*, trans. with a commentary, by Vladimir Nabokov (New York, 1964), 3:32.

7. *The Eye* (New York, 1965), p. 10.

8. *Playboy,* pp. 39 - 40.

9. *Eugene Onegin*, 1:8.

10. *Gogol*, p. 140.

11. "What Vladimir Nabokov thinks of his work, his life," interview by Peter Duval Smith, *Vogue*, March 1, 1963, p. 155.

Chapter One

1. *Eugene Onegin*, 2:353.

2. Nicholas Garnham, "The Strong Opinions of Vladimir Nabokov," an interview in *The Listener*, October 10, 1968, p. 464.

3. *The Song of Igor's Campaign*, trans. Vladimir Nabokov (New York, 1960), pp. 78 - 79.

4. Appel (Dembo), p. 32.

5. *Gogol*, p. 119.

6. Louis D. Rubin, Jr., "The Self Recaptured," *The Kenyon Review*, 25 (Summer 1963), 403.

7. Andrew Field, *Nabokov: His Life in Art* (Boston, 1967), p. 315.

8. *Speak, Memory,* (New York, 1966). All succeeding quotations in this chapter from *Speak, Memory* are noted in parentheses.

9 *Pale Fire* (New York, 1962), pp. 68 - 69.

10. *Eugene Onegin,* 3:201.

11. See *Gogol, p. 11.*

12. *Lolita* (New York, 1955 [1958]), pp. 318 - 19.

13. Appel (Dembo), p. 32.

14. *Playboy,* p. 40.

15. *The Annotated Lolita,* ed. with preface, introduction and notes by Alfred Appel, Jr. (New York, 1970), pp. 327 - 28.

16. *Poems and Problems* (New York, 1970), p. 156.

17. *Playboy,* p. 37.

18. Appel (Dembo), p. 21.

19. Page Stegner, ed. *The Portable Nabokov* (New York, 1968), p. xxxvii.

20. *The Gift,* translated from the Russian by Michael Scammell with the collaboration of the author (New York: Capricorn Books, 1970), p. 10.

21. *Annotated Lolita,* p. 424.

22. *Lolita,* pp. 318 - 19.

23. *Playboy,* p. 40.

24. *Bend Sinister,* with a new introduction by the author (New York: Time Incorporated, 1964), p. xi.

25. Vladimir Nabokov, "Anniversary Notes," Supplement to *TriQuarterly* 17, (1970), 7.

26. Appel (Dembo), pp. 19 - 20.

27. *Eugene Onegin,* 3:160.

28. *The Gift,* p. 351.

29. *Playboy,* p. 39; see also *Vogue,* p. 154.

30. *Annotated Lolita,* p. 332.

31. *Poems and Problems,* p. 45.

32. Khodasevich, p. 100.

33. *Pnin* (New York, 1957), p. 159.

34. *Poems* (New York, 1959), pp. 19 - 20.

Chapter Two

1. Field, p. 144.

2. *Tyrants Destroyed and Other Stories* (New York, 1975), p. 58.

3. *Nabokov's Dozen* (London, 1959), p. 4. All succeeding references to this work in this chapter are within parentheses in the text.

4. Appel (Dembo), p. 37.

5. *Lolita,* p. 318.

6. *Speak, Memory,* pp. 287 - 88.

7. *Mary* (New York, 1970), p. xii. All succeeding page references to *Mary* are in parentheses in context.

8. *Conclusive Evidence* (New York, 1951), p. 217.

9. Field, p. 125.

10. *King, Queen, Knave* (New York, 1968), p. vii. All succeeding page references to this novel are in parentheses.

Chapter Three

1. *The Defense* (New York, 1964), p. 10. All succeeding page references to this novel are in parentheses.

2. Khodasevich, p. 99.

3. Vladimir Nabokov, *Glory* (New York, 1971), pp. 49 - 51. All succeeding page references to this novel in Section II, only, will be noted in parentheses.

Chapter Four

1. Vladimir Nabokov, *Laughter in the Dark* (Norfolk, Connecticut, 1938), p. 7. All succeeding page references to this novel in Section I, only, will be noted in parentheses.

2. These lines from the Russian have been translated by Vladimir Milicic.

3. Dabney Stuart, *"Laughter in the Dark;* dimensions of parody," *TriQuarterly,* 17, Winter, 1970, 73.

4. Gerald Clarke, interviewer, "Checking in with Vladimir Nabokov," *Esquire,* 84, no. 1 (July 1975), 69.

5. Vladimir Nabokov, *Despair,* (New York, 1966), p. 7. All succeeding page references to this novel in Section II, only, will be noted in parentheses.

6. Khodasevich, pp. 99 - 100.

7. Claire Rosenfield, *"Despair* and the Lust for Immortality," Dembo, p. 71.

8. *Eugene Onegin,* 3:498.

9. *Invitation to a Beheading* (New York, 1959), p. 7. All page references to this novel are noted in parentheses.

10. Appel (Dembo), p. 24.

11. *Speak, Memory,* p. 139.

12. Robert Alter, *"Invitation to a Beheading:* Nabokov and the art of politics," *TriQuarterly,* 17.

13. Appel (Dembo), p. 34.

Chapter Five

1. Field, p. 249.

2. *Speak, Memory,* p. 280.

3. *The Gift* (New York, 1970), p. 10. All succeeding page references to this novel are noted in parentheses.

4. Field, pp. 241, 247.

5. Ibid., p. 244.

6. D. S. Mirsky, *A History of Russian Literature from its Beginnings to 1900* (New York; Vintage Books, 1958), p. 225.

Chapter Six

1. *The Real Life of Sebastian Knight* (Norfolk, Connecticut; 1941 [1959 edition]), p. 90. All succeeding page references to this novel are noted in parentheses.

2. Conrad Brenner, "Introduction," 1959 edition, p. xiii.

3. Ibid., p. x.

4. Charles Nicol, "The Mirrors of Sebastian Knight," Dembo, p. 86.

5. *Gogol*, p. 70.

6. *Conclusive Evidence*, p. 217.

7. *Bend Sinister* (New York, 1947), p. 58. All succeeding page references are noted in parentheses.

8. *Lolita*, p. 316.

9. *Gogol*, p. 150.

10. *Sebastian Knight*, p. 84.

11. *Gogol*, p. 149.

12. *Speak, Memory*, pp. 264 - 65.

13. *Lolita*, p. 315.

14. *Eugene Onegin*, 2:195.

15. *Gogol*, p. 29.

16. Ibid., p. 54.

17. Sir Edwin Durning-Lawrence, Bart., *Bacon is Shake-Speare* (New York, 1910), p. 23.

18. *Eugene Onegin*, 1:50.

19. *Pnin*, p. 186.

20. *Eugene Onegin*, 2:246.

21. *Bend Sinister*, Time Reading Program Edition, p. xiii.

Chapter Seven

1. *Poems and Problems*, p. 147.

2. Appel (Dembo), p. 44.

3. Smith, *Vogue*, p. 154.

4. *Poems and Problems*, p. 147.

5. *Lolita* (New York, 1955), p. 33. All succeeding page references to this novel are noted in parentheses.

6. *Playboy*, p. 36.

7. Field, p. 328.

8. *The Gift*, p. 198.

9. F. W. Dupee, "A Preface to *Lolita*," *The Anchor Review*, Number Two (Garden City, New York), 1957, p. 7.

10. Page Stegner, *Escape into Aesthetics: the Art of Vladimir Nabokov* (New York, 1966), p. 102.

11. *Playboy,* p. 36.

12. Field, p. 142.

13 Stegner, *Escape,* p. 105.

14. Appel, (Dembo), p. 30.

15. Ibid., pp. 34 - 35.

16. Appel (Dembo), p. 38.

17. Alfred Appel, Jr., "Nabokov: A Portrait," *The Atlantic Monthly,* September 1971, p. 84.

18. Ambrose Gordon, Jr., "The Double Pnin," Dembo, p. 146.

19. *Pnin* (New York, 1957), p. 7. All succeeding page references are noted in parentheses.

20. Ambrose Gordon, p. 148.

21. R. H. W. Dillard, "Not Text, But Texture: The Novels of Vladimir Nabokov," *The Hollins Critic,* 3, No. 3 (June 1966), p. 10.

22. Field, p. 132.

23. Field, p. 133.

24. *Pale Fire,* pp. 282, 155.

25. Appel (Dembo), p. 32.

26. Irwin Weil, "Odyssey of a translator," *TriQuarterly,* 17 (Winter 1970), 272.

27. *Pale Fire,* p. 192.

Chapter Eight

1. *Pale Fire* (New York, 1962). All succeeding page references to this novel are noted in parentheses.

2. Stegner, *Escape,* p. 117.

3. Appel, *Atlantic,* p. 78.

4. Mary McCarthy, "Vladimir Nabokov's *Pale Fire,*" *Encounter,* 19 (October 1962), 72.

5. *Speak, Memory,* p. 218.

6. John O. Lyons, "*Pale Fire* and the Fine Art of Annotation," Dembo, p. 157.

7. Appel (Dembo), p. 31.

8. *Eugene Onegin,* 1:8.

9. Field, p. 322.

10. *Gogol,* pp. 142, 55.

11. Appel (Dembo), p. 29.

12. *Playboy,* p. 40.

13. McCarthy, p. 81.

14. Field, p. 313.

15. *Speak, Memory,* p. 142.

16. McCarthy, p. 74.

17. Ibid., p. 82.

160

18. *Speak, Memory*, p. 218.
19. Stegner, *Escape*, p. 130.
20. Field, p. 317.
21. *Poems*, p. 22.
22. *Lolita*, p. 314.
23. *Speak, Memory*, p. 301.
24. Martin Gardner, *The Ambidextrous Universe* (New York, 1964), pp. 167 - 68, p. 177.
25. *Ada or Ardor: A Family Chronicle* (New York, 1969). All succeeding page references to this novel are noted in parentheses.
26. Appel, *Atlantic*, p. 77.
27. Northrup Frye, *An Anatomy of Criticism* (New York: Atheneum, 1967), p. 55.
28. Alfred Appel, Jr., "*Ada* described," *TriQuarterly*, 17, (Winter 1970), p. 160.

Selected Bibliography

Because Nabokov has written a great deal and because the books, monographs, articles, and reviews on his work are increasing almost every day, this bibliography is necessarily limited. Therefore, the reader's attention is called to three extensive bibliographies of Nabokov's own works: (1) Dieter E. Zimmer, *Vladimir Nabokov Bibliographie des Gesamtwerks* (Berlin: Rowohlt Verlag, 1963; 2nd ed., 1964); (2) the bibliography in Andrew Field, *Nabokov: His Life in Art* (Boston: Little, Brown and Company, 1967); and (3) Andrew Field, *Nabokov: A Bibliography* (New York: McGraw-Hill, 1973). This last bibliography by Field is by far the most complete and is the one that all Nabokov readers should consult. In L. S. Dembo, ed., *Nabokov: The Man and His Work* (Madison: University of Wisconsin Press, 1967), there is a most thorough bibliography of works about Nabokov's English books, up to 1967, compiled by Jackson R. Bryer and Thomas J. Bergin, Jr.

PRIMARY SOURCES

1. Novels and Short Stories (most of Nabokov's Russian works were published under the name V. Sirin).

Mashenka. Berlin: Slovo, 1926. Translated by Michael Glenny in collaboration with the author as *Mary.* New York: McGraw-Hill, 1970. Novel.

Korol', Dama, Valet. Berlin: Slovo, 1928. Translated by Dmitri Nabokov in collaboration with the author as *King, Queen, Knave.* New York: McGraw-Hill, 1968. Novel.

Zashchita Luzhina (Luzhin's Defense). Berlin: Slovo, 1930. Translated by Michael Scammel and Nabokov as *The Defense.* New York: G. P. Putnam's, 1964. Novel.

Vozvrashchenie Chorba (The Return of Chorb). Berlin: Slovo, 1930. Short stories.

Soglyadatay (The Spy). Published first in *Sovremennye Zapiski (Contemporary Notes* or *Annals,* an émigré journal), No. 44, 1930. Translated by Dmitri Nabokov and the author as *The Eye.* New York: Phaedra Publishers, 1965. Short novel.

161

Podvig (The Exploit). *Sovremennye Zapiski*, Paris, 1932. Translated by Dmitri Nabokov and the author as *Glory*. New York: McGraw-Hill, 1971. Novel.

Kamera Obskura (Camera obscura). *Sovremennye Zapiski*, Paris, 1932. Translated as *Camera obscura*, London: John Long, 1936. Retranslated by Nabokov as *Laughter in the Dark*. Norfolk, Connecticut: New Directions, 1938. Novel.

Otchayanie (Despair). Serialized in *Sovremennye Zapiski* in 1934; first publication in book form, Berlin: Petropolis, 1936. Translated as *Despair*. London, 1937. Retranslated by Nabokov as *Despair*. New York: G. P. Putnam's, 1966. Novel.

Soglyadatay. Paris: Russkie Zapiski, 1938. The short novel of 1930 with twelve short stories.

Priglashenie na Kazn' (Invitation to an Execution). Paris: Dom Knigi, 1938. Translated by Dmitri Nabokov and the author as *Invitation to a Beheading*. New York: G. P. Putnam's, 1959. Novel.

Dar (The Gift). First printed in *Sovremennye Zapiski*, 1937 - 1938, without the controversial fourth chapter; first publication in book form, New York: Chekhov Publishing House, 1952. Retranslated by Michael Scammell and the author as *The Gift*. New York: G. P. Putnam's, 1963. Novel.

The Real Life of Sebastian Knight. Norfolk, Connecticut: New Directions, 1941.

Nine Stories. Norfolk, Connecticut: New Directions, 1947.

Bend Sinister. New York: Henry Holt, 1947. Reprinted, with an introduction by Nabokov, in a Time Reading Program Special Edition, New York: Time Incorporated, New York, 1964. Novel.

Lolita. Paris: Olympia Press, 1955; New York: G. P. Putnam's, 1958. Novel.

Vesna v Fialte i drugie rasskazy (Spring in Fialta and Other Stories). New York: Chekhov Publishing House, 1956.

Pnin. New York: Doubleday, 1957. Novel.

Nabokov's Dozen. New York: Doubleday, 1958. Thirteen Stories.

Pale Fire. New York: G. P. Putnam's, 1962. Novel.

Nabokov's Quartet. New York: Phaedra Publishers, 1966. Short Stories.

Lolita. New York: Phaedra Publishers, 1967. Translation of *Lolita* into Russian.

Ada. New York: McGraw-Hill, 1969. Novel.

Transparent Things. New York: McGraw-Hill, 1972. Novel.

A Russian Beauty. Translated by Dmitri Nabokov and Simon Karlinsky in collaboration with the author. New York, McGraw-Hill, 1973. Short Stories.

Look at the Harlequins! New York: McGraw-Hill, 1974. Novel.

Tyrants Destroyed and Other Stories. Translated by Dmitri Nabokov in collaboration with the author. New York: McGraw-Hill, 1975. Short Stories.

2. Poems. Several collections of verse not listed here have been published plus many uncollected poems. Field's bibliography is exhaustive.

Poems. St. Petersburg: Privately printed, 1916. Russian verse.

The Empyrean Path. Berlin: Grani, 1923. Russian verse.

Poems 1929 - 1951. Paris: Rifma, 1952. Russian verse.

Poems. Garden City, New York: Doubleday, 1959. English verse.

Poems and Problems. New York: McGraw-Hill, 1970. Translations of Russian poems from 1917 to 1967; English poems of the preceding collection; chess problems.

3. Essays and Interviews

Strong Opinions. New York: McGraw-Hill, 1973. Collection of pieces, mostly essays and interviews.

4. Memoirs

Conclusive Evidence. New York: Harper & Brothers, 1951. First version of *Speak, Memory.*

Drugie berega (Other Shores). New York: Chekhov Publishing House, 1954. Expanded Russian version of *Conclusive Evidence.*

Speak, Memory: An Autobiography Revisited. New York: G. P. Putnam's, 1966. Expansion of both *Conclusive Evidence* and *Drugie berega.*

5. Drama. Nabokov has written all or parts of nine plays, plus a screenplay for *Lolita*; but only one play and the screenplay are at present available in English.

Izobretenie Val'sa ("the invention of Vals"). *Russkie Zapiski*, November, 1938. Translated by Dmitri Nabokov and the author as *The Waltz Invention.* New York: Phaedra, 1966.

Lolita: A Screenplay. New York: McGraw-Hill, 1974.

6. Translations. Nabokov has translated, mostly poetry, into and from Russian, English, and French.

Anya v strane chudes (Alice in Wonderland). Berlin: Gamaiun, 1923.

Three Russian Poets: Translations of Pushkin, Lermontov, and Tiutchev. Norfolk, Connecticut: New Directions, 1944.

A Hero of Our Time. Novel by Mihail Lermontov. Translated by Nabokov in collaboration with Dmitri Nabokov. Garden City, New York: Doubleday, 1958.

The Song of Igor's Campaign. Translated from the Old Russian. New York: Random House, 1960.

Eugene Onegin. By Aleksandr Pushkin. Bollingen Series. 4 vols. New York: Pantheon Books, 1964.

7. Recording

Lolita and Poems Read by Vladimir Nabokov. New Rochelle, New York: Spoken Arts, n.d.

164 VLADIMIR NABOKOV

SECONDARY SOURCES

1. Books

APPEL, ALFRED, JR., ed. *The Annotated Lolita.* New York: McGraw-Hill, 1970. Includes complete text of *Lolita* and a most complete, informative, and delightful set of notes by Appel — the kind of scholarship called for by most of Nabokov's .works.

————, and NEWMAN, CHARLES. eds. *Nabokov: Criticisms, Reminiscences, Translations, and Tributes.* Evanston, Illinois: Northwestern University Press, 1970. Originally published in *TriQuarterly* 17 (Winter 1970). Mixed bag of articles about Nabokov, some of which, such as the essay by Vladimir Khodasevich, are brilliant.

————. *Nabokov's Dark Cinema.* New York: Oxford University Press, 1974. Discussion of the American cinema, its effect upon the American culture, and Nabokov's use of the American cinema and culture.

BADER, JULIA. *Crystal Land: Artifice in Nabokov's English Novels.* Berkeley, California: University of California Press, 1972. Based on the idea that all of Nabokov's English novels are about art.

DEMBO. L. S., ed. *Nabokov: The Man and His Work.* Madison, Wisconsin: University of Wisconsin Press, 1967. Articles included originally published in *Wisconsin Studies in Contemporary Literature*, 8, no. 2 (Spring 1967). Articles, by various hands, and the bibliography make this one of the most useful of books for the Nabokov reader.

FOWLER, DOUGLAS. *Reading Nabokov.* Ithaca, New York: Cornell University Press, 1974. Adequate introduction to Nabokov's themes.

LOKRANTZ, JESSIE THOMAS. *The Underside of the Weave: Some Stylistic Devices Used by Vladimir Nabokov.* Uppsala, Sweden: Acta Universitatis Upsaliensis, 1973. Clear but restricted examination of Nabokov's stylistics.

FIELD, ANDREW. *Nabokov: His Life in Art.* Boston: Little, Brown and Company, 1967. Surveys the whole corpus of Nabokov's work (in Russian and English). Excellent book; best yet done on Nabokov.

MASON, BOBBIE ANN. *Nabokov's Garden: A Guide to* Ada. Ann Arbor, Michigan: Ardis Publishers, 1974. Argues that *Ada* is centered upon Van Veen's guilt for his incest.

MORTON, DONALD E. *Vladimir Nabokov.* Modern Literature Monographs. New York: Frederick Ungar, 1974. Introduction to Nabokov's themes.

MOYNAHAN, JULIAN. *Vladimir Nabokov.* University of Minnesota Pamphlets on American Writers, no. 96. Minneapolis: University of Minnesota Press, 1971. Intelligent but short introduction to Nabokov.

PROFFER, CARL. ed. *A Book of Things About Vladimir Nabokov.* Ann Arbor, Michigan: Ardis Publishers, 1973. Another mixed bag; some of the articles are charming.

————. *Keys to Lolita.* Bloomington, Indiana: Indiana University Press, 1968. Very useful set of notes on and a chronology of events in *Lolita*.

Rowe, William Woodin. *Nabokov's Deceptive World.* New York: New York University Press, 1971. On Nabokov's use of language.

Stegner, Page. *Escape into Aesthetics: The Art of Vladimir Nabokov.* Apollo Editions. New York: William Morrow, 1966. Limited to the novels originally written in English.

————, ed. *The Portable Nabokov* (originally published as *Nabokov's Congeries*). New York: Viking Press, 1971. Collection of Nabokov's works plus an introduction.

2. Essays. The reader should consult the two following bibliographies: (1) L. S. Dembo, ed. *Nabokov: The Man and His Work.* (Madison, Wisconsin: University of Wisconsin Press, 1967); (2) Blake Nevius, comp., *The American Novel: Sinclair Lewis to the Present*, Goldentree Bibliographies (New York: Meredith Corporation, 1970). The few essays noted below are among the most useful.

Appel, Alfred, Jr. "Nabokov's Puppet Show," *New Republic*, January 14, 1967, pp. 27 - 30, and Jan. 21, 1967, pp. 25 - 32. Beginning as a review of *Speak, Memory*, this essay becomes an excellent introduction to Nabokov's fiction.

Dillard, R. H. W. "Not Text, But Texture: The Novels of Vladimir Nabokov," *Hollins Critic* 3, no. 3 (June 1966), 1 - 12. Short but brilliant introduction to Nabokov's novels through *Pale Fire*.

Khodasevich, Vladislav. "On Sirin," *TriQuarterly* (Winter 1970), 96 - 101. This short article, part of a longer article written in 1937, was the first to point out that Nabokov's central theme is the act of the artist.

Lee, L. L. "Vladimir Nabokov's Great Spiral of Being," *Western Humanities Review* 18 (Summer 1964), 225 - 36. Argues that the image of the spiral draws together Nabokov's ideas of time and space and gives form to his novels.

McCarthy, Mary. "A Bolt from the Blue," *New Republic*, June 4, 1962, pp. 21 - 27. The first good reading of *Pale Fire*.

Williams, Carol T. " 'Web of Sense': *Pale Fire* in the Nabokov Canon." *Critique* 6 (Winter 1963), 29 - 45. Relates the spiral image to *Pale Fire*.

3. Interviews.

Appel, Alfred, Jr. "An Interview with Vladimir Nabokov." In *Nabokov: The Man and His Work*, edited by L. S. Dembo, pp. 19 - 44. Madison, Wisconsin: University of Wisconsin Press, 1967.

"Playboy Interview: Vladimir Nabokov." *Playboy*, January, 1964, pp. 35 - 41, 44 - 45.

Smith, Peter Duval. "What Vladimir Nabokov thinks of his work, his life." *Vogue*, March 1, 1963, pp. 152 - 55.

Index

(The works of Nabokov are listed under his name)